PUBLISHED FOR THE MALONE SOCIETY BY
OXFORD UNIVERSITY PRESS

GREAT CLARENDON STREET, OXFORD OX2 6DP

Oxford   New York
Athens   Auckland   Bangkok   Bogotá   Buenos Aires   Calcutta
Cape Town   Chennai   Dar es Salaam   Delhi   Florence   Hong Kong   Istanbul
Karachi   Kuala Lumpur   Madrid   Melbourne   Mexico City   Mumbai
Nairobi   Paris   São Paulo   Singapore   Taipei   Tokyo   Toronto   Warsaw
and associated companies in
Berlin   Ibadan

ISBN 0 19 729039 6

Printed by BAS Printers Limited, Over Wallop, Hampshire

ROMEO AND JULIET
1597

THE MALONE SOCIETY
REPRINTS, VOL. 163
2000

This edition of *Romeo and Juliet* (1597) was prepared by Jill L. Levenson and Barry Gaines and checked by Thomas L. Berger and G. R. Proudfoot.

The Society is grateful to the Huntington Library, California, for permission to reproduce its copy of the book (69361).

September 1999   THOMAS L. BERGER

© *The Malone Society 2000*

INTRODUCTION

The first quarto edition of *Romeo and Juliet* (Q1) states on its title page that it was 'Printed by Iohn Danter.|1597.'[1] It uses one of Danter's ornaments immediately above this claim.[2] Q1 collates A–K4 (A1, presumably blank, is missing from all known copies). The title page is on A2; A2^v is blank. 'The Prologue.' appears on A3; A3^v is blank. The text begins on A4 and concludes on K4 (K4^v is blank). Running titles begin on A4^v and conclude on K4. Neither this quarto nor the second (1599) was entered in the Stationers' Register.[3]

Five copies of the first quarto are known to survive.[4]

COPIES COLLATED

British Library, C.34.k.55; lacks A1; B&P 1102
Bodleian Library, Malone, 37; lacks A1; B&P 1101
Trinity College Cambridge, Capell R.20.2; lacks A1; B&P 1105
Folger Shakespeare Library, STC 22322; lacks A1, A2 (title page), A3, H2–3, I4, and K1–3 are in facsimile; outer and/or lower margins of all leaves repaired, with some lines in facsimile; B&P 1103
Henry E. Huntington Library, 69361; lacks A1; B&P 1104

Collation has revealed no variants.[5] In view of the small sample, this result does not seem particularly anomalous, and Q1 is not unique among the short

---

[1] W. W. Greg, *A Bibliography of the English Printed Drama to the Restoration* (London, 1939–59), 4 vols., i. 234 (no. 143); STC 22322.

[2] R. B. McKerrow, *Printers' & Publishers' Devices in England & Scotland, 1485–1640* (London, 1913), no. 281.

[3] Only two entries for *Romeo and Juliet* occur in the Stationers' Register, both recording rights to transfers of the play in its longer version: the first, from Cuthbert Burby to Nicholas Ling, 22 January 1607, includes *Love's Labour's Lost* and *The Taming of a Shrew*; the second, from Nicholas Ling to John Smethwick, 19 November 1607, includes *Hamlet*, *The Taming of a Shrew*, *Love's Labour's Lost*, and twelve other books. Facsimiles of these entries can be found in S. Schoenbaum, *William Shakespeare: Records and Images* (London, 1981), p. 216, plate 124, and p. 217, plate 126.

[4] Listed in Greg, *Bibliography*, i. 234, and in Henrietta C. Bartlett and Alfred W. Pollard, *A Census of Shakespeare's Plays in Quarto: 1594–1709* (New Haven, 1939), pp. 99–100, hereafter abbreviated as B&P.

[5] Barry Gaines and Jill L. Levenson independently collated the five extant copies. Unless otherwise noted, line numbers throughout the Introduction refer to those in the inner margin of the photofacsimile: that is, they are the Through Line Numbers of the first quarto (Q/TLN).

('bad') Shakespeare quartos: collation has uncovered no variants in the three copies of *2 Henry VI* (*The First Part of the Contention*) (1594) or the five copies of *The Merry Wives of Windsor* (1602).[6] There is thus no evidence in these three cases to show whether or not compositors unlocked the formes to make stop-press corrections. The typesetting errors in Q1 are unremarkable in kind and number, fewer than in the longer 1599 quarto (Q2), believed to contain a more authoritative text of the play.[7]

*

Since J. P. Collier (1842), editors and scholars have given Q1 a bad reputation, which has delayed serious investigation of its printing history. As Kirschbaum demonstrates, scholars have used documentary evidence of Danter's problems with the law to rationalize their disappointment in the literary quality of Q1.[8] The resulting arguments have distorted assessments of the quarto's authenticity as well as of its printing. Pollard, who first categorized Shakespeare's quartos as 'good' and 'bad', identified Q1 as bad on the grounds that it had no entry in the Stationers' Register and because it diverges pervasively from the Folio text, more than once calling it a 'piracy', surreptitiously published.[9]

The non-entrance of Q1 in the Stationers' Register, like its collation, constitutes negative evidence: it says nothing about Danter's right to print and publish the play or about the way he acquired the manuscript from which he

---

[6] Thomas L. Berger, 'Press Variants in Substantive Shakespearian Dramatic Quartos', *The Library*, 6th ser. x (1988), 235.

[7] These errors have been itemized and evaluated by Frank G. Hubbard in his edition of Q1, *University of Wisconsin Studies in Language and Literature* 19 (Madison, 1924), pp. 4–7, citing an earlier list by F. G. Fleay, 'The Text of *Romeo and Juliet*', *Macmillan's Magazine*, 36 (1877), 196; Harry R. Hoppe has also evaluated the errors in *The Bad Quarto of 'Romeo and Juliet': A Bibliographical and Textual Study* (Ithaca, New York, 1948), pp. 8–9. Despite the claim in its title page to be '*Newly corrected, augmented, and amended*', Q2 contains many more printing errors than Q1.

[8] Leo Kirschbaum, *Shakespeare and the Stationers* (Columbus, Ohio, 1955), p. 298.

[9] Alfred W. Pollard, *Shakespeare Folios and Quartos: A Study in the Bibliography of Shakespeare's Plays 1594–1685* (London, 1909), pp. 65, 69. The notion of clandestine publishing derives, of course, from Heminge and Condell's address in the First Folio '*To the great Variety of Readers*', where they say that they have replaced 'diuerse stolne, and surreptitious copies, maimed, and deformed by the frauds and stealthes of iniurious impostors.' (Here and throughout the Introduction, long '*s*' has been normalized.) Plomer also describes this quarto as very badly printed (H. R. Plomer, 'The Printers of Shakespeare's Plays and Poems', *The Library*, 2nd ser. vii [1906], 153, and R. B. McKerrow, *A Dictionary of Printers and Booksellers . . . 1557–1640* [London, 1910], p. 84). Plomer's claim that 'The compositors' work was of the worst description, reversed letters and mis-readings being sprinkled over every page' cannot be substantiated.

had Q1 printed.[10] The textual variations between Q1 and the longer texts printed in Q2 and the Folio (reprinted from a copy of Q3 [1609], itself a reprint of Q2) cast no light on the circumstances of its publication and furnish no evidence about the origins of the text printed as Q1.

Only the book itself gives any information about the way it was printed. Variation in type, setting, running titles, and printing conventions shows that two houses divided the printing of Q1. Danter's completed forty per cent of the book, while Edward Allde's printed sixty per cent.[11] H. R. Hoppe, the first scholar to identify Allde as the second printer, calculated that signatures A–D contain thirty-two lines to a page in roman and italic pica measuring about ninety-five millimetres for twenty lines, while signatures E–K contain thirty-six lines to a page in roman and italic long primer measuring only about eighty-two millimetres for twenty lines. The first four gatherings end neatly at the bottom of D4^v; there is no crowding or spacing out to make the text fit the pages. By contrast, the next six gatherings, E–K, which also end neatly on the last page, are noticeably spread out by spacing (between stage directions and text, at tops and bottoms of pages) or by rows of ornaments across the pages (beginning on G2^v). McKerrow was the first to remark that this spacing out spreads the text in Allde's signatures E–K to fill as many pages as they would have required had Danter's larger type of A–D been used. In addition, after D the running titles change from *The most excellent Tragedie, | of Romeo and Iuliet.* to *The excellent Tragedie | of Romeo and Iuliet.* Other features of house style, such as the treatment of proper names in stage directions, also differentiate the work of the two printers.[12]

Hoppe proposed that Danter and Allde worked on Q1 consecutively, Allde finishing the job after 'Danter's type and two presses were seized and ordered

---

[10] Both Kirschbaum, pp. 89–91, and Schoenbaum, p. 205, discuss the connection between entrance in the Stationers' Register and the right to publish; Maureen Bell gives the latest statistics for 'Entrance in the Stationers' *Register*', *The Library*, 6th ser. xvi (1994), 50–4. Regarding the rights to *Romeo and Juliet* in particular, more than one scholar has suggested that Burby, the publisher of Q2, may have been involved in the publication of Q1 or may have acquired the rights later from Danter's widow (see, for example, Hubbard, p. 9, Hoppe, pp. 13–15, and Kirschbaum, pp. 263–4). No documentary evidence supports either hypothesis.

[11] Hoppe tentatively identified the second printer as Allde (p. 3, n. 2). Standish Henning supported this attribution with additional typographical evidence in 'The Printer of "Romeo and Juliet", Q1', *Papers of the Bibliographical Society of America*, lx (1966), 363–4. Chiaki Hanabusa has demonstrated Allde's collaboration by re-examining damaged types. See 'Edward Allde's Types in Sheets E–K of *Romeo and Juliet* Q1 (1597)', *Papers of the Bibliographical Society of America*, 91 (1997), 423–8.

[12] See Hoppe's first chapter, 'The Printing of the First Quarto', especially pp. 1–4, 41–4, and R. B. McKerrow, 'The Treatment of Shakespeare's Text by His Earlier Editors, 1709–1768', *Annual Shakespeare Lecture of the British Academy* (London, 1933), p. 33, n. 6.

to be defaced on 10 Apr. 1597.'[13] Hoppe believed that the compositors in both printing shops set pages seriatim. However, shortages, recurrence, and distribution of type, as well as habits of spelling and the use of spacing materials, indicate that both A–D and E–K were cast off and set by formes.[14] Danter's employment of Allde implies a wish to accelerate production by using two printing shops and working not consecutively, as Hoppe supposed, but concurrently. In short, Q1 is a typical printing job shared by two London printing houses. Initial casting off in Danter's printing house would explain not only the tidy completion of D but also the spacing out of E–K.[15] In studies since Hoppe's, bibliographers have supported his conclusion that two compositors set E–K; and Haggard has shown that outer B, C, and D probably went through the press before their inner formes.[16]

Danter must have divided the work with Allde to speed production by using the resources of two printing houses working simultaneously.[17] The date on the title page, if reliable, indicates that the quarto was printed at some time in 1597. In an attempt to make this time-frame more specific, scholars have urged the calendar (rather than the legal) year, using two facts to argue for early 1597: a raid by the Stationers' Company on Danter's shop sometime during Lent, 9 February–27 March, and the title-page reference to 'the L. of *Hunsdon* his Seruants', the name of Shakespeare's company only from 22 July 1596–17 April 1596/7.[18] According to these arguments, the raid closed Danter's printing house, leaving Allde to finish the printing of Q1. In fact, however, both Danter and Allde were subject to disciplinary action by the Stationers' Company at the same time and for similar misde-

---

[13] Greg, *Bibliography*, i. 234, see Hoppe, pp. 38–52. Hoppe first published this theory in 'An Approximate Printing Date for the First Quarto of *Romeo and Juliet*', *The Library*, 4th ser. xviii (1938), 447–55.

[14] Several studies use such evidence to establish how Q1 was printed: George Walton Williams, 'Setting by Formes in Quarto Printing', *Studies in Bibliography*, xi (1958), 52–3; Henning, op. cit.; Frank E. Haggard, 'Type-Recurrence Evidence and the Printing of *Romeo and Juliet* Q1 (1597)', *Papers of the Bibliographical Society of America*, lxxi (1977), 66–73; and W. Craig Ferguson, 'Compositor Identification in *Romeo* Q1 and *Troilus*', *Studies in Bibliography*, xlii (1989), 212–14.

[15] J. A. Lavin notes the implications of casting off for this shared printing of Q1 in 'John Danter's Ornament Stock', *Studies in Bibliography*, xxiii (1970), 33–4.

[16] Hoppe, pp. 46–56, assembled evidence for Compositors X and Y; Williams and Ferguson provided corroboration (Williams suggesting that X set outer formes first). Haggard analysed the work of the compositors on the entire quarto.

[17] In *A New Introduction to Bibliography*, 1972 (Oxford, 1978), p. 168, Philip Gaskell offers possible reasons for the division of printing between shops. For a wider range of possibilities, see Peter W. M. Blayney, *The Texts of 'King Lear' and their Origins*, vol. 1 (Cambridge, 1982), pp. 49–52.

[18] Chiaki Hanabusa, 'A Neglected Misdate and *Romeo and Juliet* Q1 (1597)', *Notes and Queries*, N.S. xlvi (1999), 229–30.

meanours. The *Records* cite Allde immediately after Danter ('Whereas alsoe latelie') for printing a Catholic volume, and they note defacement of the offending 'peece of presse and lres' [letters = type].[19] Although Danter might have printed all three of his known 1597 books before mid-March, one of them, *Mihil Mumchance, his discouerie of the art of cheating in false dyce play* (STC 17916), was entered only on 22 August (entrance usually suggesting at least completion of printing, if not imminent publication). Danter also printed at least one book in 1598, Richard Johnson's *The pilgrimage of man, wandering in a wilderness of woe* (STC 14691.1), before Simon Stafford purchased his stock. Allde's shop remained productive throughout 1597.

The printed reference to Lord Hunsdon's Servants on the Q1 title page need have no implications for dating its printing. The information may have been inaccurate, or the reference may have been up-to-date when written but out-of-date when the book was printed some months later. A date of publication for Q1 *Romeo and Juliet* early in 1597 is neither proven nor disproven by the facts cited as evidence.[20]

*

Arguments about the nature and origins of the printer's copy for Q1 *Romeo and Juliet* inevitably depend on comparisons between the texts published in the first and second quartos. Such arguments are necessarily speculative because of the lack of other documentary evidence. These speculations depend on four aspects of the first two quartos: the dates on their title pages which indicate that Q1 was printed before Q2; the claim on the title page of Q2 that its text is '*Newly corrected, augmented, and amended*' (A1); the differences between the two texts in length and expression; and the close verbal and typographic correspondence of Q2 to Q1 in one long segment (Q/TLN 224–317), as well as in a number of shorter ones.[21] In length, Q1 is close to seventy-nine per cent as long as Q2 (2,364 lines compared with just over 3,000 lines). It contains over 800 lines which in some identifiable ways correspond to lines in the longer text.[22] It also includes several passages

---

[19] *Records of the Court of the Stationers' Company, 1576 to 1602, from Register B*, ed. W. W. Greg and E. Boswell (London, 1930), pp. 56–7. Danter's offending book was an edition of the Psalter of Jesus (STC 14567). Allde's was *A briefe forme of confession* (STC 11181).

[20] In a private communication to the editors, Blayney summarized the two printers' output during the relevant period and concluded that 'neither the fact of the raid nor the description of the company's action constitutes proof that the book was actually printed before the raid.'

[21] Kathleen O. Irace, *Reforming the 'Bad' Quartos: Performance and Provenance of Six Shakespearean First Editions* (Newark, Delaware; New York, London, and Toronto, 1994), pp. 101, 178.

[22] See Hoppe, pp. 181–4, 189–90.

which differ completely from their equivalents in Q2 (for example, II. vi: Q/TLN 1079–1110; IV. v. 43–70: Q/TLN 1972–86; V. iii. 13–17: Q/TLN 2127–32).[23] Yet Q1 served as printer's copy for Q2 at least once, from Q/TLN 224–317.[24] Q2, apparently elsewhere printed from authorial working papers,[25] follows this Q1 passage in wording, use of upper-case letters, punctuation, spelling, and typography, in particular the odd use of italics for the speeches of the Nurse.[26] It appears that the Q2 printers also consulted Q1 elsewhere (for instance, II. i. 13: Q/TLN 577–8; II. iv. 101–3: Q/TLN 951–4; III. v. 27–31: Q/TLN 1551–5).[27] Consequently, bibliographers in general agree that Q1 influenced Q2, but the exact nature and extent of that influence remain uncertain.[28]

These aspects of the relation between Q1 and Q2 have given rise to three theories about the character of the printers' copy for Q1 and about the influence of Q1 on Q2. Arguments for memorial reconstruction may be said to have become the modern orthodoxy. The concept of memorial transmission, originated by Tycho Mommsen in 1857, supported with varying degrees of

---

[23] Act, scene, and line numbers cited in the Introduction are from the Riverside edition of Shakespeare (ed. G. B. Evans, *et al.* [Boston, 1974, 1997], pp. 1055–99, 1101–45).

[24] The exact limits of the passage may be impossible to fix. This edition follows that of George Walton Williams (Durham, North Carolina, 1964), p. 105.

[25] Evidence of revision, in the form of first and second thoughts preserved in the printed text, argues that Q2 was close to a manuscript draft in Shakespeare's hand. Although editors and bibliographers are now in general agreement about the nature of the printer's copy for Q2, the matter was much debated until the 1950s. The theory that Thomas Creede printed Q2 from Shakespeare's own manuscript but consulted Q1 was first proposed by Robert Gericke in '*Romeo and Juliet* nach Shakespeare's Manuscript', *Shakespeare Jahrbuch*, xiv (1879), 207–73; G. Hjort argued for the opposite view, that Q2 was printed from a copy of Q1 collated with a manuscript; see 'The Good and Bad Quartos of "Romeo and Juliet" and "Love's Labour's Lost"', *Modern Language Review*, xxi (1926), 140–6.

[26] Greg's summary of the use of italics in both quartos in 'Principles of Emendation in Shakespeare', *Annual Shakespeare Lecture of the British Academy* (London, 1928), pp. 49–50, suggested that the Q1 compositor might have set type from a manuscript or actor's part in an Italian hand. See also, W. W. Greg, *The Shakespeare First Folio: Its Bibliographical and Textual History* (Oxford, 1955), p. 226. Jay L. Halio proposes that Danter may have been short of type in 'Handy-Dandy: Q1/Q2 *Romeo and Juliet*', in *Shakespeare's 'Romeo and Juliet': Texts, Contexts, and Interpretation*, ed. Jay L. Halio (Newark, Delaware, and London, 1995), p. 150, n. 47.

[27] See Brian Gibbons's New Arden edition of *Romeo and Juliet* (London and New York, 1980), pp. 21–3, for a survey of scholarship on these bibliographical links.

[28] Most discussions of this issue use Pollard's idiom, as does Richard Hosley in 'The Corrupting Influence of the Bad Quarto on the Received Text of *Romeo and Juliet*', *Shakespeare Quarterly*, iv (1953), 11–33. Jonathan Goldberg adopts a different idiom and point of view to discuss the subject in '"What? in a names that which we call a Rose", The Desired Texts of *Romeo and Juliet*', in *Crisis in Editing: Texts of the English Renaissance,* ed. Randall McLeod (New York, 1994), pp. 173–201.

confidence by Greg over four decades, and endorsed by much recent scholarship, has received wide acceptance since Hoppe's book made its case in 1948.[29] The theory holds that an actor or actors, perhaps disaffected or out of work, reproduced the play from memory, either for production (possibly by the revived Pembroke's company or on provincial tour) or for publication. The play reported may have been a variant form of the *Romeo and Juliet* represented by Q2, perhaps abridged and otherwise adapted for provincial performance by Shakespeare's company. The play reported may have been the official acting version of *Romeo and Juliet*. Alternatively, it may have been an unofficial conflation of the abridged acting text and the longer play represented by Q2. The actor(s) would have remembered this original from taking part in a performance of it or from reading a copy of it in manuscript. Memory, perhaps assisted by actors' parts or portions of a manuscript, may have faltered, such lapses accounting for the shortness of the Q1 text. What is most difficult to explain in terms of the fallibility of memory is the extent to which the 'reported' Q1 corresponds with the 'authentic' Q2. One solution is to posit variable quality of reporting. This is achieved by nominating as reporters the actors who might have produced the largest number of matching lines. The possibilities range from those who played Capulet, the Nurse, and Benvolio to those who played Romeo, Paris, and Mercutio.[30]

In 1987 *A Textual Companion* to The Oxford Shakespeare supported arguments for memorial reconstruction as a means of transmitting playtexts. However, since the 1970s and especially in the 1990s, the case for this

---

[29] Mommsen first published his version of the theory in '"Hamlet", 1603; and "Romeo and Juliet", 1597', *The Athenaeum*, xxix (1857), 182. Greg's accounts of memorial reconstruction appear in his edition *Shakespeare's 'Merry Wives of Windsor' 1602* (Oxford, 1910), xxvi–xli; *Two Elizabethan Stage Abridgements: 'The Battle of Alcazar' & 'Orlando Furioso'* (Oxford, 1922), pp. 256–60; 'Principles of Emendation in Shakespeare', pp. 40–1; *The Editorial Problem in Shakespeare: A Survey of the Foundations of the Text* (Oxford, 1942), pp. xxiv, 9, 62–4; and *The Shakespeare First Folio*, pp. 225–6. Kathleen O. Irace offers a recent endorsement in *Reforming the 'Bad' Quartos* (1994), *passim*. In addition to works already cited, significant contributions to the debate were made by J. Dover Wilson and A. W. Pollard, 'The "Stolne and Surreptitious" Shakespearian Texts. *Romeo and Juliet*, 1597', *Times Literary Supplement*, 14 August 1919, p. 434; Leo Kirschbaum, 'A Census of Bad Quartos', *Review of English Studies*, xiv (1938), 20–43, and 'An Hypothesis Concerning the Origin of the Bad Quartos', *PMLA*, lx (1945), 697–715; and Alfred Hart, *Stolne and Surreptitious Copies: A Comparative Study of Shakespeare's Bad Quartos* (Melbourne and London, 1942), pp. 341–51.

[30] Another theory of reporting maintains that either a stenographer in the audience took the play down in shorthand or a hack writer made longhand notes of a performance. Robert E. Burkhart summarizes the brief, unsuccessful history of the stenographic theory in *Shakespeare's Bad Quartos: Deliberate Abridgments Designed for Performance by a Reduced Cast* (The Hague and Paris, 1975), pp. 10–11.

method has been challenged on several grounds.[31] First, no documentary evidence survives to verify that any actor(s) ever reconstructed a play memorially; and it seems unlikely that reporters would have forgotten their own lines and cues during the time of the play's theatrical currency. Second, the logic behind a few assumptions about memorial reconstruction seems dubious. For example, some advocates of memorial reconstruction have considered the play-texts in question corrupt, their states reflected by their illegitimate appropriation and piratical publication. They presume on commercial grounds both that a stationer would have bought such a play without qualms and that a printer would happily have manufactured it as a book, with tacit permission of the players and without protest from the purchasers.[32] But no documentary evidence confirms that any play was ever stolen from Shakespeare's company. Moreover, whatever the risks, not only to the actor(s) but also to the stationer and printer, the returns would have been small. Playbooks did not make high profits under even the most legitimate circumstances. Peter W. M. Blayney proposes a 'commonplace and innocent origin' for anomalous play-texts. He points out that Humphrey Moseley's address to the readers of the first Beaumont and Fletcher Folio (1647) makes reference to actors preparing copies of plays for their friends, usually from versions abridged for performance, writing down what had been spoken on stage. The quality of such texts would vary according to the actors' sources and procedures.[33]

Two further dissenting views provide different explanations for Q1 copy and the relationship of the quartos. Alexander Pope introduced the idea that Shakespeare revised and enlarged early versions of his plays, a concept prevalent during the nineteenth century and supported by a small but growing number of scholars since the 1980s.[34] According to this theory, Q1 of *Romeo and Juliet* would be seen as a first draft for Q2. Conversely, a few

---

[31] See Gary Taylor's General Introduction to *A Textual Companion* (Oxford, 1987), pp. 23–8. The opposing views represented in this introduction are from Burkhart, pp. 19–22; Paul Werstine, 'Narratives about Printed Shakespeare Texts: "Foul Papers" and "Bad" Quartos', *Shakespeare Quarterly*, xli (1990), 65–86; David Bradley, *From Text to Performance in the Elizabethan Theatre: Preparing the Play for the Stage* (Cambridge, 1992), pp. 9–11; Halio, pp. 123–50; and David Farley-Hills, 'The "Bad" Quarto of *Romeo and Juliet*', *Shakespeare Survey*, 49 (1996), 27–44.

[32] According to *A Textual Companion*, p. 26, texts of Shakespeare's plays diverging widely from those now considered authoritative were not published between 1609 and his death in 1616.

[33] See 'The Publication of Playbooks', in *A New History of Early English Drama*, ed. John D. Cox and David Scott Kastan (New York, 1996), pp. 383–422.

[34] See Hoppe, pp. 58–64, for a history of the concept to 1948; Irace, pp. 95–114, devotes a chapter to the general topic of revision and the return to this hypothesis in recent years by scholars such as Steven Urkowitz.

scholars have argued that Q1 is a deliberate abridgement of Q2, made by a redactor (or even by Shakespeare himself) from a holograph closely resembling the copy for Q2.[35] This view emphasizes the efficiency of cuts which pare down poetic and rhetorical passages to accelerate the action, producing a quickly paced, popular version of the play for performance whether on a provincial tour or in London. This view of Q1 allows for the preservation in it of some Shakespearian revisions. In this view, some stage directions may reflect the redactor's experience of the uncut play in performance. Whatever course revision may have taken, Q1 thus acquires a measure of authority. These last two views accept as intentional the differences between Q1 and Q2, the hundreds of variations which make the extant texts seem like two forms of the same play. The Q2 title page, with its promise of a tragedy '*Newly corrected, augmented, and amended*', does not, the argument goes, repudiate Q1 but rather acknowledges its own connection with an alternative version of the play authorized by Shakespeare's company.

Fourteen years after Pollard made the distinction between good and bad quartos, Greg indicated the awkwardness with which it fitted the two substantive texts of Shakespeare's early tragedy: '... *Romeo and Juliet* is remarkable in that the bad text seems a good deal better, and the good text a good deal worse, than we are accustomed to find.'[36] The relationship between these two quartos is unusually puzzling, because Q1 shows signs of a theatrical provenance that Q2 appears to lack. As a result, the bibliographical connection between Q1 and Q2 may involve not only the processes of composition, transcription, printing, and perhaps memory, but also theatrical interventions of various kinds. As Paul Werstine surmised, the early theatrical history of *Romeo and Juliet* may be embedded in the first quarto: 'It is relatively easy to distinguish the possible stages of such a history in abstract terms. . . . Yet it seems quite optimistic to believe that such raw stuff as this quarto . . . will readily yield up to rational analysis the record of theatrical process that it contains.'[37] It is probably just as unlikely that Q1 will ever give an unambiguous account of the play's early textual career.

*

The present reproduction is a 1:1 photofacsimile prepared from photographs of the Stace-Kemble-Devonshire copy in the Henry E. Huntington

---

[35] The most extensive such studies are by Burkhart (in his chapter on *Romeo and Juliet*, pp. 55–67), Halio, and Farley-Hills.

[36] 'Principles of Emendation in Shakespeare', p. 23.

[37] 'The First Quarto of *Romeo and Juliet* and the Limits of Authority', typescript of a paper delivered at the 1985 meeting of the Society for Textual Scholarship, pp. 10–11.

Library, San Marino, California.[38] In Appendix II of *Shakespeare's Plays in Quarto*, Michael J. B. Allen and Kenneth Muir list thirty-eight readings which they consider unclear.[39]

*

This edition contains two forms of line reference:
1. In the inner margins are Through Line Numbers to the Quarto (Q/TLN), beginning with the title on A2. Catchwords are not included in the count.[40]
2. In the outer margins are Through Line Numbers for the text of *Romeo and Juliet* as it appears in the 1623 Folio (F/TLN) and as it is reproduced and numbered by Charlton Hinman in *The Norton Facsimile: The First Folio of Shakespeare*.[41] The number of every tenth line in F/TLN is placed opposite its corresponding line in the Quarto.

---

[38] CSmH, Huntington 69361, B&P 1104. This copy was purchased by Huntington in January, 1914. It had belonged to John Philip Kemble, who wrote 'Collated & Perfect, J.P.K. 1809' (see B&P, p. 107).
The Malone Society acknowledges with gratitude the permission given by the Henry E. Huntington Library to prepare this facsimile. The Society is grateful to the Library's Rare Book Librarian, Thomas Lange, for his many considerations, and to Michael J. B. Allen, the late Kenneth Muir, and the University of California Press for the loan of photographs used in the preparation of their *Shakespeare's Plays in Quarto* (Berkeley, Los Angeles, and London, 1981).

[39] p. 891. Their difficult readings in this facsimile include: thrust (Q/TLN 44), subiects (Q/TLN 75), siedge (Q/TLN 172), surreuerence loue (Q/TLN 369), smelling out a sute, (Q/TLN 403), Children (Q/TLN 420), and (Q/TLN 428), reuels, and (Q/TLN 432), life, closde (Q/TLN 433), some vntimelie forfet (Q/TLN 434), Forsweare (Q/TLN 469), *Ti:* It fits (Q/TLN 491), You'le make (Q/TLN 496), wilfull choller meeting, (Q/TLN 503), flesh (Q/TLN 504), vnworthie (Q/TLN 507), shrine, (Q/TLN 508), shewes (Q/TLN 512), lips (Q/TLN 516), let (Q/TLN 517), haue tooke. (Q/TLN 523), *Ladie of the* (Q/TLN 529), *can* (Q/TLN 531), Sunne, (Q/TLN 607), but farewell complements. (Q/TLN 690), loue (Q/TLN 724), tale (Q/TLN 945), *Prince,* (Q/TLN 1227), art (Q/TLN 1235), Thursday (Q/TLN 1507), feare (Q/TLN 1808), troe (Q/TLN 1927), starued (Q/TLN 2085), from (Q/TLN 2241), come, come. (Q/TLN 2242), vs (Q/TLN 2265), *Juliet* (Q/TLN 2295). Muir and Allen list '*Exit*' as an unclear reading on H2, between Q/TLN 1720 and 1721. Rather, it is show-through from 'Heere' at Q/TLN 1749 on H2ᵛ.
The following readings in this facsimile may also be difficult: Ile thrust (Q/TLN 44), enuie (Q/TLN 1296), little (Q/TLN 1368), from (Q/TLN 1376), a Diuine, a ghostly (Q/TLN 1383), beare (Q/TLN 1388), banished, (Q/TLN 1390), Banished? hang (Q/TLN 1391), *Juliet* (Q/TLN 1392), reuerse a Princes doome, (Q/TLN 1393), teare (Q/TLN 1403), is (Q/TLN 1435), *hearbs* (Q/TLN 1909), Logs (Q/TLN 1924), choose dryer (Q/TLN 1925), fetch (Q/TLN 1926), lambe (Q/TLN 1938), sticke (Q/TLN 1990), *They all but the Nurse goe foorth, casting* (Q/TLN 1996), *a mattocke* (Q/TLN 2135), cosen (Q/TLN 2163), pursued further (Q/TLN 2165), condemnes thee (Q/TLN 2167), be gone, tempt (Q/TLN 2169).

[40] The one exception to this is Q/TLN 338, '*Enter Clowne.*', a stage direction that constitutes the catchword for B4ᵛ but which does not appear as such as the first line of C1.

[41] New York, 1968 and 1996, pp. 669–93.

Hyphenated numbers are placed alongside single Quarto lines which contain something more than one Folio line (as with Q/TLN 154, which appears as two lines, F/TLN 201–2, in the Folio). A bracket indicates that two or more Quarto lines are printed as a single line in the Folio (as with Q/TLN 88–9, which appear as F/TLN 105 in the Folio).

Where the Quarto lacks something more than a word or phrase which appears in the Folio, the F/TLN of the last line before the omitted material is entered at the appropriate place and is followed immediately by the F/TLN of the first line after it (for example, F/TLN 998 is followed by F/TLN 1003, because at this point there are four lines in the Folio which do not appear in the Quarto). Where the Quarto contains material which is not in the Folio, this is signalled by a plus sign, + (as with Q/TLN 348–50, lines which are not fully represented in the Folio text).[42]

On pp. 79–80 below, there is a table of correspondences between the Quarto signatures, page numbers in the present edition, Quarto Through Line Numbers, and the act, scene, and line numbers which are given for *Romeo and Juliet* in *The Riverside Shakespeare*.[43]

The Appendix at pp. 81–91 contains supplementary pages from the copy in the Library of Trinity College Cambridge, reproduced by kind permission of the Master and Fellows of Trinity College. The nine pages here reproduced supplement the Huntington Library copy where its pages are impaired by shine-through or cropping. Damage and dirt elsewhere in the Trinity College copy unhappily render it unsuitable for use as the sole basis of a facsimile.

---

[42] Charlton Hinman introduced and explained this system in his Shakespeare Quarto Facsimiles of *Much Ado About Nothing* (Oxford, 1971), pp. x–xiii, and *Othello* (Oxford, 1975), pp. xii–xiv.

[43] pp. 1055–99, pp. 1101–45. Marvin Spevack's *Complete and Systematic Concordance to the Works of Shakespeare*, vols. 1–6 (Hildesheim, 1968–70), is based on the Riverside text, as is his later *Harvard Concordance to Shakespeare* (Cambridge, Mass., 1973).

AN
EXCELLENT
conceited Tragedie
OF
Romeo and Iuliet.

As it hath been often (with great applause)
plaid publiquely, by the right Honourable the L. of *Hunsdon*
his Seruants.

LONDON,
Printed by Iohn Danter.
1597.

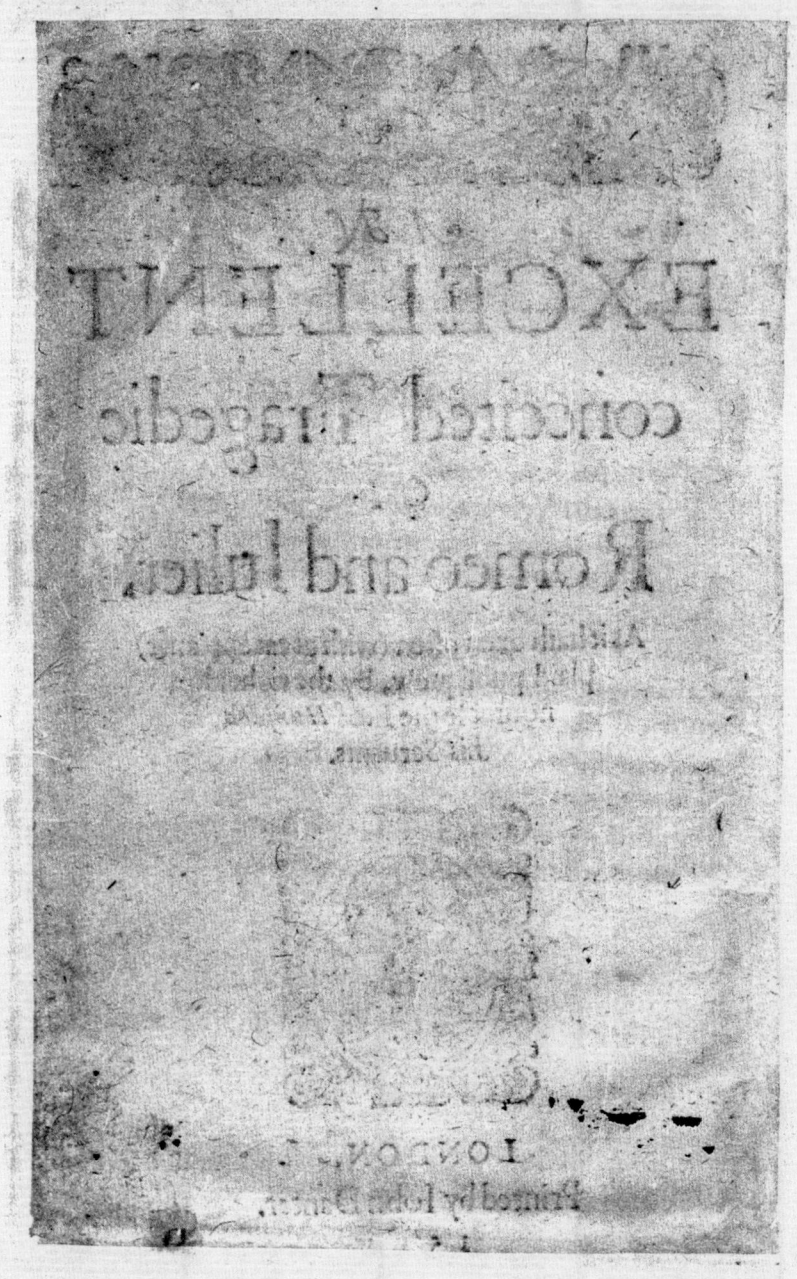

The Prologue.

TVVo houshold Frends alike in dignitie,
(In faire Verona, where we lay our Scene)
From ciuill broyles broke into enmitie,
VVhose ciuill warre makes ciuill hands vncleane.
From forth the fatall loynes of these two foes,
A paire of starre-crost Louers tooke their life:
VVhose misaduentures, piteous ouerthrowes,
(Through the continuing of their Fathers strife,
And death-markt passage of their Parents rage)
Is now the two howres traffique of our Stage.
The which if you with patient eares attend,
VVhat here we want wee'l studie to amend.

The Prologue.

Two houshold Friends alike in dignitie,
(In fayre Verona, where we lay our Scene)
From ciuill broyles broke into enmitie,
Whose ciuill warre makes ciuill hands vncleane.
From forth the fatall loynes of these two foes,
A paire of starre-crost Louers tooke their life:
Whose misaduentures, piteous ouerthrowes,
(Through the continuing of their Fathers strife,
And death-markt passage of their Parents rage)
Is now the two howres traffique of our Stage.
The which if you with patient eares attend,
What here we want wee'l studie to amend.

The most excellent Tragedie of
Romeo and Iuliet.

Enter 2. Seruing-men of the Capolets.

G *Regorie,* of my word Ile carrie no coales.
   2 No, for if you doo, you should be a Collier.
   1 If I be in choler, Ile draw.
   2 Euer while you liue, drawe your necke out of the
the collar.
   1 I strike quickly being moou'd.
   2 I, but you are not quickly moou'd to strike.
   1 A Dog of the house of the *Mountagues* moues me.
   2 To mooue is to stirre, and to bee valiant is to stand
to it: therefore (of my word) if thou be mooud thou't
runne away.
   1 There's not a man of them I meete, but Ile take
the wall of.
   2 That shewes thee a weakling, for the weakest goes
to the wall.
   1 Thats true, therefore Ile thrust the men from the
wall, and thrust the maids to the walls: nay, thou shalt
see I am a tall peece of flesh.
   2 Tis well thou art not fish, for if thou wert thou
wouldst be but poore Iohn.
   1 Ile play the tyrant, Ile first begin with the maids, &
off with their heads.
   2 The heads of the maids?

1 I,

The most excellent Tragedie,

1 I the heades of their Maides, or the Maidenheades,
take it in what sence thou wilt.

2 Nay let them take it in sence that feele it, but heere
comes two of the *Mountagues.*

Enter two Seruingmen of the Mountagues.

1 Nay feare not me I warrant thee.

2 I feare them no more than thee, but draw.

1 Nay let vs haue the law on our side, let them begin
first. Ile tell thee what Ile doo, as I goe by ile bite my
thumbe, which is disgrace enough if they suffer it.

2 Content, goe thou by and bite thy thumbe, and ile
come after and frowne.

1 *Moun:* Doo you bite your thumbe at vs?

1 I bite my thumbe.

2 *Moun:* I but i'st at vs?

1 I bite my thumbe, is the law on our side?

2 No.

1 I bite my thumbe.

1 *Moun:* I but i'st at vs? *Enter Beneuolio.*

2 Say I, here comes my Masters kinsman.

They draw, to them enters Tybalt, *they fight, to them the
Prince, old* Mountague, *and his wife, old* Capulet *and
his wife, and other Citizens and part them.*

Prince Rebellious subiects enemies to peace,
On paine of torture, from those bloody handes
Throw your mistempered weapons to the ground.
Three Ciuell brawles bred of an airie word,
By the old *Capulet* and *Mountague,*
Haue thrice disturbd the quiet of our streets.
If euer you disturbe our streets againe,

Your

of Romeo and Iuliet.

Your liues shall pay the ransome of your fault:
For this time euery man depart in peace.
Come *Capulet* come you along with me,
And *Mouutague*, come you this after noone,
To know our farther pleasure in this case,
To old free Towne our common iudgement place,
Once more on paine of death each man depart.
         Exeunt.

 M: wife. Who set this auncient quarrel first abroach?
Speake Nephew, were you by when it began?
 Benuo: Here were the seruants of your aduersaries,
And yours close fighting ere I did approch.
 VVife: Ah where is *Romeo*, saw you him to day?
Right glad I am he was not at this fray.
 Ben: Madame, an houre before the worshipt sunne
Peept through the golden window of the East,
A troubled thought drew me from companie:
Where vnderneath the groue *Sicamoure*,
That Westward rooteth from the Cities side,
So early walking might I see your sonne.
I drew towards him, but he was ware of me,
And drew into the thicket of the wood:
I noting his affections by mine owne,
That most are busied when th'are most alone,
Pursued my honor, not pursuing his.
 Moun: Black and portentious must this honor proue,
Vnlesse good counsaile doo the cause remooue.
 Ben: Why tell me Vncle do you know the cause?
     Enter Romeo.
 Moun: I neyther know it nor can learne of him.
 Ben: See where he is, but stand you both aside,
Ile know his grieuance, or be much denied.
    B   *Mount:*

The most excellent Tragedie,

Mount: I would thou wert so happie by thy stay
To heare true shrift. Come Madame lets away.
  Benuo: Good morrow Cosen.
  Romeo: Is the day so young?
  Ben: But new stroke nine.
  Romeo: Ay me, sad hopes seeme long.
Was that my Father that went hence so fast?
  Ben: It was, what sorrow lengthens *Romeos* houres?
  Rom: Not hauing that, which hauing makes them
  Ben: In loue.   (short.
  Ro: Out.
  Ben: Of loue.
  Ro: Out of her fauor where I am in loue.
  Ben: Alas that loue so gentle in her view,
Should be so tyrranous and rough in proofe.
  Ro: Alas that loue whose view is muffled still,
Should without lawes giue path-waies to our will:
Where shall we dine? Gods me, what fray was here?
Yet tell me not for I haue heard it all,
Heres much to doe with hate, but more with loue.
Why then, O brawling loue, O louing hate,
O anie thing, of nothing first create!
O heauie lightnes serious vanitie!
Mishapen *Caos* of best seeming thinges,
Feather of lead, bright smoke, cold fire, sicke health,
Still waking sleepe, that is not what it is:
This loue feele I, which feele no loue in this.
Doest thou not laugh?
  Ben: No Cose I rather weepe.
  Rom: Good hart at what?
  Ben: At thy good hearts oppression.
  Ro: Why such is loues transgression,
                                            Griefes

of Romeo and Iuliet.

Griefes of mine owne lie heauie at my hart,
Which thou wouldst propagate to haue them prest
With more of thine, this griefe that thou hast showne,
Doth ad more griefe to too much of mine owne:
Loue is a smoke raisde with the fume of sighes
Being purgde, a fire sparkling in louers eyes:
Being vext, a sea raging with a louers teares.
What is it else? A madnes most discreet,
A choking gall, and a preseruing sweet. Farewell Cose.
   Ben: Nay Ile goe along.
And if you hinder me you doo me wrong.
   Ro: Tut I haue lost my selfe I am not here,
This is not *Romeo*, hee's some other where.
   Ben: Tell me in sadnes whome she is you loue?
   Ro: What shall I grone and tell thee?
   Ben: Why no, but sadly tell me who.
   Ro: Bid a sickman in sadnes make his will.
Ah word ill vrgde to one that is so ill.
In sadnes Cosen I doo loue a woman.
   Ben: I aimde so right, when as you said you lou'd.
   Ro: A right good mark-man, and shee's faire I loue.
   Ben: A right faire marke faire Cose is soonest hit.
   Ro: But in that hit you misse, shee'le not be hit
With *Cupids* arrow, she hath *Dianaes* wit,
And in strong proofe of chastitie well arm'd:
Gainst *Cupids* childish bow she liues vnharm'd,
Shee'le not abide the siedge of louing tearmes,
Nor ope her lap to Saint seducing gold,
Ah she is rich in beautie, only poore,
That when she dies with beautie dies her store. *Exeu.*
      Enter Conntie Paris, *old* Capulet.
Of honorable reckoning are they both,

B 2   And

The most excellent Tragedie,

And pittie tis they liue at ods so long:
But leauing that, what say you to my sute?
   Capu: What should I say more than I said before,
My daughter is a stranger in the world,
Shee hath not yet attainde to fourteene yeares:
Let two more sommers wither in their pride,
Before she can be thought fit for a Bride.
   Paris: Younger than she are happie mothers made.
   Cap: But too soone marde are these so early maried:
But wooe her gentle *Paris*, get her heart,
My word to her consent is but a part.
This night I hold an old accustom'd Feast,
Whereto I haue inuited many a guest,
Such as I loue: yet you among the store,
One more most welcome makes the number more.
At my poore house you shall behold this night,
Earth treadding stars, that make darke heauen light:
Such comfort as doo lusty youngmen feele,
When well apparaild Aprill on the heele
Of limping winter treads, euen such delights
Amongst fresh female buds shall you this night
Inherit at my house, heare all, all see,
And like her most, whose merite most shalbe.
Such amongst view of many myne beeing one,
May stand in number though in reckoning none.
               Enter Seruingman.
Where are you sirra, goe trudge about
Through faire *Verona* streets, and seeke them out:
Whose names are written here and to them say,
My house and welcome at their pleasure stay.
                            Exeunt.
   Ser: Seeke them out whose names are written here,
                                       and

of Romeo and Iuliet.

and yet I knowe not who are written here: I must to
the learned to learne of them, that's as much to say, as
the Taylor must meddle with his Laste, the Shoomaker
with his needle, the Painter with his nets, and the Fisher
with his Pensill, I must to the learned.

Enter Benuolio and Romeo.

Ben: Tut man one fire burnes out anothers burning,
One paine is lessned with anothers anguish:
Turne backward, and be holp with backward turning,
One desperate griefe cures with anothers languish.
Take thou some new infection to thy eye,
And the ranke poyson of the old will die.

Romeo: Your Planton leafe is excellent for that.

Ben : For what?

Romeo: For your broken shin.

Ben : Why *Romeo* art thou mad?

Rom: Not mad, but bound more than a mad man is.
Shut vp in prison, kept without my foode,
Whipt and tormented, and Godden good fellow.

Ser: Godgigoden, I pray sir can you read,

Rom : I mine owne fortune in my miserie.

Ser : Perhaps you haue learned it without booke:
but I pray can you read any thing you see?,

Rom : I if I know the letters and the language.

Seru: Yee say honestly, rest you merrie.

Rom: Stay fellow I can read.

He reads the Letter.

SEigneur Martino *and his wife and daughters, Countie*
Anselme *and his beauteous sisters, the Ladie widdow of*
Vtruuio, *Seigneur* Placentio, *and his louelie Neeces,*
Mercutio *and his brother* Valentine *, mine vncle* Capu-
let *his wife and daughters , my faire Neece* Rosaline *and*

B 3   *Liuia*

The most excellent Tragedie,

Liuia, Seigneur Valentio *and his Cosen* Tibalt, Lucio *and the liuelie* Hellena.
A faire assembly, whether should they come?
　Ser: Vp.
　Ro: Whether to supper?
　Ser: To our house.
　Ro: Whose house?
　Ser: My Masters.
　Ro: Indeed I should haue askt thee that before.
　Ser: Now il'e tel you without asking. My Master is the great rich *Capulet*, and if you be not of the house of *Mountagues*, I pray come and crush a cup of wine. Rest you merrie.
　Ben: At this same auncient feast of *Capulets*,
Sups the faire Rosaline whom thou so loues:
With all the admired beauties of *Verona*,
Goe thither and with vnattainted eye,
Compare her face with some that I shall shew,
And I will make thee thinke thy swan a crow.
　Ro: When the deuout religion of mine eye
Maintaines such falshood, then turne teares to fire,
And these who often drownde could neuer die,
Transparent Heretiques be burnt for liers.
One fairer than my loue, the all seeing sonne
Nere saw her match, since first the world begun.
　Ben: Tut you saw her faire none els being by,
Her selfe poysd with her selfe in either eye:
But in that Cristall scales let there be waide,
Your Ladyes loue, against some other maide
That I will shew you shining at this feast,
And she shall scant shew well that now seemes best.
　Rom: Ile goe along no such sight to be showne,

But

of Romeo and Iuliet.

But to reioyce in splendor of mine owne.
Enter Capulets wife and Nurce.

 VVife: Nurce wher's my daughter call her forth to mee.

 Nurce: *Now by my maiden head at twelue yeare old I bad her come, what Lamb, what Ladie bird, God forbid. VVher's this girle? what* Iuliet.   *Enter Iuliet.*

 Iuliet: How now who cals?

 Nurce: *Your Mother.*

 Iul: Madame I am here, what is your will?

 VV: This is the matter, Nurse giue leaue a while, we must talke in secret, Nurce come back again I haue remembred me, thou'se heare our counsaile. Thou knowest my daughters of a prettie age.

 Nurce: *Faith I can tell her age vnto a houre.*

 VVife: Shee's not fourteene.

 Nurce: *Ile lay fourteene of my teeth, and yet to my teene be it spoken, I haue but foure, shee's not fourteene. How long is it now to* Lammas-tide?

 VVife: A fortnight and odde dayes.

 Nurce: *Euen or odde, of all dayes in the yeare come* Lammas *Eue at night shall she be fourteene.* Susan *and she God rest all Christian soules were of an vge. VVell* Susan *is with God, she was too good for me: But as I said on* Lammas *Eue at night shall she be fourteene, that shall she marie I remember it well. Tis since the Earth-quake nowe eleauen yeares, and she was weand I neuer shall forget it, of all the daies of the yeare vpon that day: for I had then laid wormewood to my dug, sitting in the sun vnder the Douehouse wall. My Lord and you were then at* Mantua, *nay I do beare a braine: But as I said, when it did taft the wormwood on the nipple of my dug, & felt it bitter, pretty foole*

to

13

The most excellent Tragedie,

to see it teachie and fall out with Dugge. Shake quoth the
Doue-house twas no need I trow to bid me trudge, and since
that time it is a leauen yeare: for then could Iuliet stande
high lone, nay by the Roode, shee could haue wadled vp and
downe, for euen the day before shee brake her brow, and then
my husband God be with his soule, hee was a merrie man:
Dost thou fall forward Iuliet? thou wilt fall backward when
thou hast more wit: wilt thou not Iuliet? and by my holli-
dam, the pretty foole left crying and said I. To see how a
ieast shall come about, I warrant you if I should liue a hundred yeare, I neuer should forget it, wilt thou not Iuliet?
and by my troth she stinted and cried I.

 Iuliet: And stint thou too, I pre thee Nurce say I.

 Nurce: *VVell goe thy waies, God marke thee for his
grace, thou wert the prettiest Babe that euer I nurst, might
I but liue to see thee married once, I haue my wish.*

 VVife: And that same marriage Nurce, is the Theame
I meant to talke of: Tell me *Iuliet*, howe stand you af-
fected to be married?

 Iul: It is an honor that I dreame not off.

 Nurce: *An honor! were not I thy onely Nurce, I
would say thou hadst suckt wisedome from thy Teat.*

 VVife: Well girle, the Noble Countie *Paris* seekes
thee for his Wife.

 Nurce: *A man young Ladie, Ladie such a man as all
the world, why he is a man of waxe.*

 VVife: *Veronaes* Summer hath not such a flower.

 Nurce: *Nay he is a flower, in faith a very flower.*

 VVife: Well *Iuliet*, how like you of *Paris* loue.

 Iuliet: Ile looke to like, if looking liking moue,
But no more deepe will I engage mine eye,
Then your consent giues strength to make it flie.

Enter Clowne.

of Romeo and Iuliet.

Clowne: *Maddam you are cald for, supper is readie,*
the Nurce curst in the Pantrie, all thinges in extreamitie,
make hast for I must be gone to waite.

Enter Maskers with Romeo and a Page.

Ro: What shall this speech bee spoke for our excuse?
Or shall we on without Apologie.

Benuoleo: The date is out of such prolixitie,
Weele haue no *Cupid* hudwinckt with a Scarfe,
Bearing a *Tartars* painted bow of lath,
Scaring the Ladies like a crow-keeper:
Nor no without booke Prologue faintly spoke
After the Prompter, for our entrance.
But let them measure vs by what they will,
Weele measure them a measure and be gone.

Rom: A torch for me I am not for this aumbling,
Beeing but heauie I will beare the light.

Mer: Beleeue me *Romeo* I must haue you daunce.

Rom: Not I beleeue me you haue dancing shooes
With nimble soles, I haue a soule of lead
So stakes me to the ground I cannot stirre.

Mer: Giue me a case to put my visage in,
A visor for a visor, what care I
What curious eye doth coate deformitie.

Rom: Giue me a Torch, let wantons light of hart
Tickle the senceles rushes with their heeles:
For I am prouerbd with a Grandsire phrase,
Ile be a candleholder and looke on,
The game was nere so faire and I am done.

Mer: Tut dun's the mouse, the Cunstables old word,
If thou beest Dun, weele draw thee from the mire
Of this surreuerence loue wherein thou stickst.
Leaue this talke, we burne day light here.

C **Rom:** Nay

The most excellent Tragedie,

497–8	*Rom:* Nay thats not so. *Mer:* I meane sir in delay,
	Weburne our lights by night, like Lampes by day,
500	Take our good meaning for our iudgement sits
	Three times a day, ere once in her right wits.
	Rom: So we meane well by going to this maske,
	But tis no wit to goe.
	Mer: Why *Romeo* may one aske?
505	*Rom:* I dreamt a dreame to night.
506–7	*Mer:* And so did I. *Rom:* Why what was yours?
	Mer: That dreamers often lie.
	Rom: in bed asleepe while they doe dreame things true.
510	*Mer:* Ah then I see Queene Mab hath bin with you,
510+	*Ben:* Queene Mab whats she?
511	She is the Fairies Midwife and doth come
511–12	In shape no bigger than an Aggat stone
512	On the forefinger of a Burgomaster,
513	Drawne with a teeme of little Atomi,
513–14	Athwart mens noses when they lie asleepe.
514–15	Her waggon spokes are made of spinners webs,
515	The couer, of the winges of Grashoppers,
515–17	The traces are the Moone-shine wattrie beames,
517–18	The collers crickets bones, the lash of filmes,
518–19	Her waggoner is a small gray coated flie,
519	Not halfe so big as is a little worme,
520	Pickt from the lasie finger of a maide,
522–3	And in this sort she gallops vp and downe
523–4	Through Louers braines, and then they dream of loue
524–5	O're Courtiers knees: who strait on cursies dreame
526	O're Ladies lips, who dreame on kisses strait:
526–7	Which oft the angrie Mab with blisters plagues,
527–8	Because their breathes with sweet meats tainted are:
528–9, 525	Sometimes she gallops ore a Lawyers lap,
	And

	380
	390
	400

And then dreames he of smelling out a sute,
And sometime comes she with a tithe pigs taile,
Tickling a Parsons nose that lies a sleepe,
And then dreames he of another benefice:
Sometime she gallops ore a souldiers nose,
And then dreames he of cutting forraine throats,
Of breaches ambuscados, counter mines,
Of healthes fiue fadome deepe, and then anon
Drums in his eare, at which he starres and wakes,
And sweares a Praier or two and sleepes againe.
This is that Mab that makes maids lie on their backes,
And proues them women of good cariage: (the night,
This is the verie Mab that plats the manes of Horses in
And plats the Elfelocks in foule sluttish haire,
Which once vntang'led much misfortune breedes.

   Rom: Peace, peace, thou talkst of nothing.

   Mer: True I talke of dreames,
Which are the Children of an idle braine,
Begot of nothing but vaine fantasie,
Which is as thinne a substance as the aire,
And more inconstant than the winde,
Which wooes euen now the frose bowels of the north,
And being angred puffes away in haste,
Turning his face to the dew-dropping south.

   Ben: Come, come, this winde doth blow vs from our
Supper is done and we shall come too late.

   Ro: I feare too earlie, for my minde misgiues
Some consequence is hanging in the stars,
Which bitterly begins his fearefull date
With this nights reuels, and expiers the terme
Of a dispised life, closde in this breast,
By some vntimele forfet of vile death:

The most excellent Tragedie,

But he that hath the steerage of my course
Directs my saile, on lustie Gentlemen.
   Enter old Capulet *with the Ladies.*
 Capu: Welcome Gentlemen, welcome Gentlemen,
Ladies that haue their toes vnplagud with Corns
Will haue about with you, ah ha my Mistresses,
Which of you all will now refuse to dance?
Shee that makes daintie, shee Ile sweare hath Corns.
Am I come neere you now, welcome Gentlemen, wel
More lights you knaues, & turn these tables vp, (come,
And quench the fire the roome is growne too hote.
Ah sirra, this vnlookt for sport comes well,
Nay sit, nay sit, good Cosen *Capulet:*
For you and I are past our standing dayes,
How long is it since you and I were in a Maske?
 Cos: By Ladie sir tis thirtie yeares at least.
 Cap: Tis not so much, tis not so much.
Tis since the mariage of *Lucentio,*
Come *Pentecost* as quicklie as it will,
Some fiue and twentie yeares, and then we maske.
 Ces: Tis more, tis more, his sonne is elder far.
 Cap: Will you tell me that it cannot be so,
His sonne was but a Ward three yeares agoe,
Good youths I faith. Oh youth's a iolly thing.
 Rom: What Ladie is that that doth inrich the hand
Of yonder Knight? O shee doth teach the torches to
     burne bright!
It seemes she hangs vpon the cheeke of night,
Like a rich iewell in an *Aethiops* eare,
Beautie too rich for vse, for earth too deare:
So shines a snow-white Swan trouping with Crowes,
As this faire Ladie ouer her fellowes showes.
          The

18

of Romeo and Iuliet.

The measure done, ile watch her place of stand,
And touching hers, make happie my rude hand.
Did my heart loue till now? forsweare it sight,
I neuer saw true beautie till this night.
   Tib: This by his voice should be a *Mountague*,
Fetch me my rapier boy. What dares the slaue
Come hither couer'd with an Anticke face,
To scorne and ieere at our solemnitie?
Now by the stocke and honor of my kin,
To strike him dead I hold it for no sin.
   Ca: Why how now Cosen, wherfore storme you so.
   Ti: Vncle this is a *Mountague* our foe,
A villaine that is hether come in spight,
To mocke at our solemnitie this night.
   Ca: Young *Romeo*, is it not?
   Ti: It is that villaine *Romeo*.
   Ca: Let him alone, he beares him like a portly gentle- (man,
And to speake truth, *Verona* brags of him,
As of a verttious and well gouern'd youth:
I would not for the wealth of all this towne,
Here in my house doo him disparagement:
Therefore be quiet take no note of him,
Beare a faire presence, and put off these frownes,
An ill beseeming semblance for a feast.
   Ti: I, when such a villaine is a guest,
Ile not indure him.
   Ca: He shalbe indured, goe to I say, he shall,
Am I the Master of the house or you?
You'le not indure him? God shall mend my soule
You'le make a mutenie amongst my guests,
You'le set Cocke a hoope, you'le be the man.
   Ti: Vncle tis a shame.
                             C 3   *Ca:* Goe

The most excellent Tragedie,

Ca: Goe too, you are a saucie knaue.
This tricke will scath you one day I know what,
Well said my hartes. Be quiet :
More light Ye knaue, or I will make you quiet. *(sing.*

Tibalt: Patience perforce with wilfull choller mee-
Makes my flesh tremble in their different greetings:
I will withdraw, but this intrusion shall
Now seeming sweet, conuert to bitter gall.

Rom: If I prophane with my vnworthie hand,
This holie shrine, the gentle sinne is this:
My lips two blushing Pilgrims ready stand,
To smooth the rough touch with a gentle kisse.

Iuli: Good Pilgrime you doe wrong your hand too
Which mannerly deuotion shewes in this: (much,
For Saints haue hands which holy Palmers touch,
And Palme to Palme is holy Palmers kisse.

Rom: Haue not Saints lips, and holy Palmers too?

Iuli: Yes Pilgrime lips that they must vse in praier.

Ro: Why then faire saint, let lips do what hands doo,
They pray, yeeld thou, least faith turne to dispaire.

Iu: Saints doe not mooue though: grant nor praier
  forsake.

Ro: Then mooue not till my praiers effect I take.
Thus from my lips, by yours my sin is purgde.

Iu: Then haue my lips the sin that they haue tooke.

Ro: Sinne from my lips, O trespasse sweetly vrgde!
Giue me my sinne againe.

Iu: You kisse by the booke.

Nurse: *Madame your mother calles.*

Rom: What is her mother?

Nurse: *Marrie Batcheler her mother is the Lady of the house, and a good Lady, and a wise, and a vertuous. I nurst*

of Romeo and Iuliet.

her daughter that you talkt withall, I tell you, he that can
lay hold of her shall haue the chinkes.

    Rom: Is she a *Mountague*? Oh deare account,
My life is my foes thrall.

    Ca: Nay gentlemen prepare not to be gone,
We haue a trifling foolish banquet towards.
                                They whisper in his eare.
I pray you let me intreat you. Is it so?
Well then I thanke you honest Gentlemen,
I promise you but for your company,
I would haue bin a bed an houre agoe:
Light to my chamber hoe.
                                          Exeunt.

    Iul: Nurse, what is yonder Gentleman?

    Nur: *The sonne and heire of old* Tiberio.

    Iul: Whats he that now is going out of dore?

    Nur: *That as I thinke is yong* Petruchio.   (dance

    Iul: Whats he that followes there that would not

    Nur: *I know not.*

    Iul: Goe learne his name, if he be maried,
My graue is like to be my wedding bed.

    Nur: *His name is* Romeo *and a* Mountague, *the onely*
       sonne of your great enemie.

    Iul: My onely Loue sprung from my onely hate,
Too early seene vnknowne, and knowne too late,
Prodigious birth of loue is this to me,
That I should loue a loathed enemie.

    Nurse: VVhats this? whats that?

    Iul: Nothing Nurse but a rime I learnt euen now of
      one I daunst with.

    Nurse: *Come your mother staies for you, Ile goe a long*
      with you.   *Exeunt.*
                                             Enter

The most excellent Tragedie,

Enter Romeo alone.

Ro: Shall I goe forward and my heart is here?
Turne backe dull earth and finde thy Center out.
            Enter Benuolio Mercutio.
Ben: Romeo, my cosen Romeo.
   Mer: Doest thou heare he is wise,
Vpon my life he hath stolne him home to bed.
   Ben: He came this way, and leapt this Orchard wall:
Call good *Mercutio.*
   Mer: Call, nay Ile coniure too.
Romeo, madman, humors, passion, liuer, appeare thou in
likenes of a sigh: speek but one rime & I am satisfied, cry
but ay me. Pronounce but Loue and Doue, speake to
my gossip *Venus* one faire word, one nickname for her
purblinde sonne and heire young *Abraham*: *Cupid* hee
that shot so trim when young King *Cophetua* loued the
begger wench. Hee heares me not. I coniure thee by
Rosalindes bright eye, high forehead, and scarlet lip, her
prettie foote, straight leg, and quiuering thigh, and the
demaines that there adiacent lie, that in thy likenesse
thou appeare to vs.

   Ben: If he doe heare thee thou wilt anger him.
   Mer: Tut this cannot anger him, marrie if one shuld
raise a spirit in his Mistris circle of some strange fashion,
making it there to stand till she had laid it, and coniurde
it downe, that were some spite. My inuocation is faire
and honest, and in his Mistris name I coniure onely but
to raise vp him.
   Ben: Well he hath hid himselfe amongst those trees,
To be consorted with the humerous night,
Blinde in his loue, and best besits the darke.

Mer

Mer: If loue be blind, loue will not hit the marke,
Now will he sit vnder a Medler tree,
And wish his Mistris were that kinde of fruite,
As maides call Medlers when they laugh alone,
Ah *Romeo* that she were, ah that she were,
An open *Et cætera*, thou a poprin Peare.
Romeo God night, i'le to my trundle bed:
This field bed is too cold for mee.
Come lets away, for tis but vaine,
To seeke him here that meanes not to be found.

   Ro: He iests at scars that neuer felt a wound:
But soft, what light forth yonder window breakes?
It is the East, and *Iuliet* is the Sunne,
Arise faire Sunne, and kill the enuious Moone
That is alreadie sicke, and pale with griefe:
That thou her maid, art far more faire than she.
Be not her maide since she is enuious,
Her vestall liuerie is but pale and greene,
And none but fooles doe weare it, cast it off.
She speakes, but she sayes nothing. What of that?
Her eye discourseth, I will answere it.
I am too bold, tis not to me she speakes,
Two of the fairest starres in all the skies,
Hauing some busines, doe entreat her eyes
To twinckle in their spheares till they returne.
What if her eyes were there, they in her head,
The brightnes of her cheekes would shame those stars:
As day-light doth a Lampe, her eyes in heauen,
Would through the airie region streame so bright,
That birdes would sing, and thinke it were not night.
Oh now she leanes her cheeke vpon her hand,
I would I were the gloue to that same hand,

                D   That

The most excellent Tragedie,

That I might kisse that cheeke.
   Iul: Ay me.
   Rom: She speakes, Oh speake againe bright Angell:
For thou art as glorious to this night beeing ouer my
As is a winged messenger of heauen   (head,
Vnto the white vpturned woondring eyes,
Of mortals that fall backe to gaze on him,
When he bestrides the lasie pacing cloudes,
And sailes vpon the bosome of the aire.
   Iul: Ah *Romeo, Romeo*, wherefore art thou *Romeo?*
Denie thy Father, and refuse thy name,
Or if thou wilt not be but sworne my loue,
And il'e no longer be a *Capulet*.
   Rom: Shall I heare more, or shall I speake to this?
   Iul: Tis but thy name that is mine enemie.
Whats *Mountague*? It is nor hand nor foote,
Nor arme, nor face, nor any other part:
Whats in a name? That which we call a Rose,
By any other name would smell as sweet:
So *Romeo* would, were he not *Romeo* cald,
Retaine the diuine perfection he owes:
Without that title *Romeo* part thy name,
And for that name which is no part of thee,
Take all I haue.
   Rom: I take thee at thy word,
Call me but loue, and il'e be new Baptisde,
Henceforth I neuer will be *Romeo*.
   Iu: What man art thou, that thus beskrind in night,
Doest stumble on my counsaile?
   Ro: By a name I know not how to tell thee.
My name deare Saint is hatefull to my selfe,
Because it is an enemie to thee,
                        Had

of Romeo and Iuliet.

Had I it written I would teare the word.

   Iul: My eares haue not yet drunk a hundred words
Of that tongues vtterance, yet I know the sound:
Art thou not *Romeo* and a *Mountague*?

   Ro: Neyther faire Saint, if eyther thee displease.

   Iu: How camst thou hether, tell me and wherfore?
The Orchard walles are high and hard to clime,
And the place death considering who thou art,
If any of my kinsmen finde thee here.

   Ro: By loues light winges did I oreperch these wals,
For stonie limits cannot hold loue out,
And what loue can doo, that dares loue attempt,
Therefore thy kinsmen are no let to me.

   Iul: If they doe finde thee they will murder thee.

   Ro: Alas there lies more perrill in thine eyes,
Then twentie of their swords, looke thou but sweete,
And I am proofe against their enmitie.

   Iul: I would not for the world they shuld find thee (here.

   Ro: I haue nights cloak to hide thee from their sight,
And but thou loue me let them finde me here:
For life were better ended by their hate,
Than death proroged wanting of thy loue.

   Iu: By whose directions foundst thou out this place.

   Ro: By loue, who first did prompt me to enquire,
He gaue me counsaile and I lent him eyes.
I am no Pilot: yet wert thou as farre
As that vast shore, washt with the furthest sea,
I would aduenture for such Marchandise.

   Iul: Thou knowst the maske of night is on my face,
Els would a Maiden blush bepaint my cheeks:
For that which thou haste heard me speake to night,
Faine would I dwell on forme, faine faine denie,

D 2   Wha

The most excellent Tragedie,

What I haue spoke: but farewell complementes,
Doest thou loue me? Nay I know thou wilt say I,
And I will take thy word: but if thou swearst,
Thou maiest proue false,
At Louers periuries they say Ioue smiles.
Ah gentle *Romeo*, if thou loue pronounce it faithfully:
Or if thou thinke I am too easely wonne,
I'le frowne and say thee nay, and be peruerse,
So thou wilt wooe: but els not for the world,
In truth faire *Mountague* I am too fond,
And therefore thou maiest thinke my hauiour light:
But trust me gentleman Ile proue more true,
Than they that haue more cunning to be strange.
I should haue bin strange I must confesse,
But that thou ouer-heardst ere I was ware
My true loues Passion: therefore pardon me,
And not impute this yeelding to light loue,
Which the darke night hath so discouered.

Ro: By yonder blessed Moone I sweare,
That tips with siluer all these fruit trees tops.

Iul: O sweare not by the Moone the vnconstant,
That monthlie changeth in her circeled orbe,
Least that thy loue proue likewise variable.

Ro: Now by

Iul: Nay doo not sweare at all,
Or if thou sweare, sweare by thy glorious selfe,
Which art the God of my Idolatrie,
And i'le beleeue thee.

Ro: If my true harts loue

Iul: Sweare not at al, though I doo ioy in thee,
I haue small ioy in this contract to night,
It is too rash, too sodaine, too vnaduisde,

Too

of Romeo and Iuliet.

Too like the lightning that doth cease to bee
Ere one can say it lightens. I heare some comming,
Deare loue adew, sweet *Mountague* be true,
Stay but a little and il'e come againe.

   Ro: O blessed blessed night, I feare being night,
All this is but a dreame I heare and see,
Too flattering true to be substantiall.

   Iul: Three wordes good *Romeo* and good night in-
If that thy bent of loue be honourable? (deed.
Thy purpose marriage, send me word to morrow
By one that il'e procure to come to thee:
Where and what time thou wilt performe that right,
And al my fortunes at thy foote il'e lay,
And follow thee my Lord through out the world.

   Ro: Loue goes toward loue like schoole boyes from
 their bookes,
But loue from loue, to schoole with heauie lookes.

   Iul: *Romeo, Romeo*, O for a falkners voice,
To lure this Tassell gentle backe againe:
Bondage is hoarse and may not crie aloud,
Els would I teare the Caue where Eccho lies
And make her airie voice as hoarse as mine,
With repetition of my *Romeos* name.
Romeo?

   Ro: It is my soule that calles vpon my name,
How siluer sweet sound louers tongues in night.

   Iul: Romeo?

   Ro: Madame.

   Iul: At what a clocke to morrow shall I send?

   Ro: At the houre of nine.

   Iul: I will not faile, tis twentie yeares till then.
Romeo I haue forgot why I did call thee backe.

D 3   *Rom:*

The most excellent Tragedie,

 Rom: Let me stay here till you remember it.
 Iul: I shall forget to haue thee still staie here,
Remembring how I loue thy companie.
 Rom: And il'e stay still to haue thee still forget,
Forgetting any other home but this.
 Iu: Tis almost morning I would haue thee gone,
But yet no further then a wantons bird,
Who lets it hop a little from her hand,
Like a pore prisoner in his twisted giues,
And with a silke thred puls it backe againe,
Too louing iealous of his libertie.
 Ro: Would I were thy bird.
 Iul: Sweet so would I,
Yet I should kill thee with much cherrishing thee.
Good night, good night, parting is such sweet sorrow,
That I shall say good night till it be morrow. (breast,
 Rom: Sleepe dwell vpon thine eyes, peace on thy
I would that I were sleep and peace of sweet to rest.
Now will I to my Ghostly fathers Cell,
His help to craue, and my good hap to tell.
   Enter Frier Francis. (night,
 Frier: The gray ey'd morne smiles on the frowning
Checkring the Easterne clouds with streakes of light,
And flecked darkenes like a drunkard reeles,
From forth daies path, and *Titans* fierie wheeles:
Now ere the Sunne aduance his burning eye,
The world to cheare, and nights darke dew to drie,
We must vp fill this oasier Cage of ours,
With balefull weeds, and precious iuyced flowers,
Oh mickle is the powerfull grace that lies
In hearbes, plants, stones, and their true qualities:
For nought so vile, that vile on earth doth liue,

              But

But to the earth some speciall good doth giue:
Nor nought so good, but straind from that faire vse,
Reuolts to vice and stumbles on abuse:
Vertue it selfe turnes vice being misapplied,
And vice sometimes by action dignified.
Within the infant rinde of this small flower,
Poyson hath residence, and medecine power:
For this being smelt too, with that part cheares ech hart,
Being tasted slaies all sences with the hart.
Two such opposed foes incampe them still,
In man as well as herbes, grace and rude will,
And where the worser is predominant,
Full soone the canker death eats vp that plant.

 Rom: Good morrow to my Ghostly Confessor.
 Fri: Benedicite, what earlie tongue so soone saluteth
Yong sonne it argues a distempered head, (me?
So soone to bid good morrow to my bed.
Care keepes his watch in euerie old mans eye,
And where care lodgeth, sleep can neuer lie:
But where vnbrused youth with vnstuft braines
Doth couch his limmes, there golden sleepe remaines:
Therefore thy earlines doth me assure,
Thou art vprowf'd by some distemperature.
Or if not so, then here I hit it righ
Our *Romeo* hath not bin a bed to night.
 Ro: The last was true, the sweeter rest was mine.
 Fr: God pardon sin, wert thou with *Rosaline*?
 Ro: With *Rosaline* my Ghostly father no,
I haue forgot that name, and that names woe. (then?
 Fri: Thats my good sonne: but where hast thou bin
 Ro: I tell thee ere thou aske it me againe,
I haue bin feasting with mine enemie:
            Where

The most excellent Tragedie,

Where on the sodaine one hath wounded mee
Thats by me wounded, both our remedies
With in thy help and holy phisicke lies,
I beare no hatred blessed man: for loe
My intercession likewise steades my foe.

  Frier: Be plaine my sonne and homely in thy drift,
Ridling confession findes but ridling shrift.
  Rom: Then plainely know my harts deare loue is set
On the faire daughter of rich *Capulet*:
As mine on hers, so hers likewise on mine,
And all combind, saue what thou must combine
By holy marriage: where, and when, and how,
We met, we woo'd, and made exchange of vowes,
Il'e tell thee as I passe: But this I pray,
That thou consent to marrie vs to day.
  Fri: Holy *S. Francis*, what a change is here?
Is *Rosaline* whome thou didst loue so deare
So soone forsooke, lo yong mens loue then lies
Not truelie in their harts, but in their eyes.
Iesu Maria, what a deale of brine
Hath washt thy sallow cheekes for *Rosaline*?
How much salt water cast away in waste,
To season loue, that of loue doth not taste.
The sunne not yet thy sighes from heauen cleares,
Thy old grones ring yet in my ancient eares,
And loe vpon thy cheeke the staine doth sit,
Of an old teare that is not washt off yet.
If euer thou wert thus, and these woes thine,
Thou and these woes were all for *Rosaline*,
And art thou changde, pronounce this sentence then
Women may fal, when ther's no strength in men.
  Rom: Thou chidst me oft for louing *Rosaline*.

Frier:

of Romeo and Iuliet.

Fr: For doating, not for louing, pupill mine.
Rom: And badst me burie loue.
Fr: Not in a graue,
To lay one in another out to haue.
Rom: I pree thee chide not, she whom I loue now
Doth grace for grace, and loue for loue allow:
The other did not so.
Fr: Oh she knew well
Thy loue did read by rote, and could not spell.
But come yong Wauerer, come goe with mee,
In one respect Ile thy assistant bee:
For this alliaunce may so happie proue,
To turne your Housholds rancour to pure loue. *Exeunt.*

Enter Mercutio, Benuolio.

Mer: Why whats become of *Romeo?* came he not
home to night?
Ben: Not to his Fathers, I spake with his man.
Mer: Ah that same pale hard hearted wench, that *Ro-*
Torments him so, that he will sure run mad. (*saline*
Mer: *Tybalt* the Kinsman of olde *Capolet*
Hath sent a Letter to his Fathers House:
Some Challenge on my life.
Ben: *Romeo* will answere it.
Mer: I, anie man that can write may answere a letter.
Ben: Nay, he will answere the letters master if hee bee
challenged.
Mer: Who, *Romeo?* why he is alreadie dead: stabd
with a white wenches blacke eye, shot thorough the eare
with a loue song, the verie pinne of his heart cleft with the
blinde bow-boyes but-shaft. And is he a man to encounter
Tybalt?
Ben: Why what is *Tybalt?*
Mer: More than the prince of cattes I can tell you. Oh
he is the couragious captaine of complements, Catso, he
E fights

The excellent Tragedie

fightes as you sing pricke-song, keepes time dystance and
proportion, rests me his minum rest one two and the thirde
in your bosome, the very butcher of a silken button, a Duellist a Duellist, a gentleman of the very first house of the first
and second cause, ah the immortall Passado, the Punto re-
uerso, the Hay.

Ben: The what?

Me: The Poxe of such limping antique affecting fan-
tasticoes these new tuners of accents. By Iesu a very good
blade, a very tall man, a very good whoore. Why graund-
sir is not this a miserable case that we should be still afflicted
with these strange flies: these fashionmongers, these par-
donmees, that stand so much on the new forme, that they
cannot sitte at ease on the old bench. Oh their bones, theyr
bones.

Ben. Heere comes *Romeo*.

Mer: Without his Roe, like a dryed Hering. O flesh flesh
how art thou fishified. Sirra now is he for the numbers that
Petrarch flowdin: *Laura* to his Lady was but a kitchin
drudg, yet she had a better loue to berime her: Dido a dow-
dy Cleopatra a Gypsie, *Hero* and *Hellen* hildings and harle-
tries: *Thisbie* a gray eye or so, but not to the purpose. Signior
Romeo bon iour, there is a French curtesie to your French
slop: yee gaue vs the counterfeit fairely yesternight.

Rom: What counterfeit I pray you?

Me: The slip the slip, can you not conceiue?

Rom: I cry you mercy my busines was great, and in such
a case as mine, a man may straine curtesie.

Mer. Oh thats as much to say as such a case as yours wil
constraine a man to bow in the hams.

Rom: A most curteous exposition.

Me: Why I am the very pinke of curtesie.

Rom: Pinke for flower?

Mer: Right.

Rom: Then is my Pumpe well flour'd.

Mer: Well said, follow me nowe that iest till thou hast
worne

of Romeo and Iuliet.

worne out thy Pumpe, that when the single sole of it is worn the iest may remaine after the wearing solie singuler.

Rom: O single soald iest solie singuler for the singlenes.

Me. Come between vs good *Benuolio,* for my wits faile.

Rom: Swits and spurres, swits & spurres, or Ile cry a match.

Mer: Nay if thy wits runne the wildgoose chase, I haue done: for I am sure thou hast more of the goose in one of thy wits, than I haue in al my fiue: Was I with you there for the goose?

Rom: Thou wert neuer with me for any thing, when thou wert not with me for the goose.

Me: Ile bite thee by the eare for that iest.

Rom: Nay good goose bite not.

Mer: Why thy wit is a bitter sweeting, a most sharp sauce

Rom: And was it not well seru'd in to a sweet goose?

Mer: Oh heere is a witte of Cheuerell that stretcheth from an ynch narrow to an ell broad.

Rom: I stretcht it out for the word broad, which added to the goose, proues thee faire and wide a broad goose.

Mer: Why is not this better now than groning for loue? why now art thou sociable, now art thou thy selfe, nowe art thou what thou art, as wel by arte as nature. This driueling loue is like a great naturall, that runs vp and downe to hide his bable in a hole.

Ben: Stop there.

Me: Why thou wouldst haue me stopp my tale against the haire.

Ben: Thou wouldst haue made thy tale too long?

Mer: Tut man thou art deceiued, I meant to make it short, for I was come to the whole depth of my tale? and meant indeed to occupie the argument no longer.

Rom: Heers goodly geare.

Enter Nurse and her man.

Mer: A saile, a saile, a saile.
    E 2   *Ben:* Two

The excellent Tragedie

Ben: Two, two, a shirt and a smocke.
Nur: Peter, pree thee giue me my fan.
Mer: Pree thee doo good *Peter*, to hide her face: for her fanne is the fairer of the two.
Nur: God ye goodmorrow Gentlemen.
Mer: God ye good den faire Gentlewoman.
Nur: Is it godye gooden I pray you.
Mer: Tis no lesse I assure you, for the baudie hand of the diall is euen now vpon the pricke of noone.
Nur: Fie, what a man is this?
Rom: A Gentleman Nurse, that God hath made for himselfe to marre.
Nur: By my troth well said : for himselfe to marre quoth he? I pray you can anie of you tell where one maie finde yong *Romeo*?
Rom: I can: but yong *Romeo* will bee elder when you haue found him, than he was when you sought him, I am the yongest of that name for fault of a worse.
Nur: Well said.
Mer: Yea, is the worst well? mas well noted, wisely, wisely.
Nu: If you be he sir, I desire some conference with ye.
Ben: O, belike she meanes to inuite him to supper.
Mer: So ho. A baud, a baud, a baud.
Rom: Why what hast found man?
Mer: No hare sir, vnlesse it be a hare in a lenten pye, that is somewhat stale and hoare ere it be eaten.

He walkes by them, and sings.

And an olde hare hore, and an olde hare hore
    is verie good meate in Lent:
But a hare thats hoare is too much for a score,
    if it hore ere it be spent.
You! come to your fathers to supper?
Rom: I will.
Mer: Farewell ancient Ladie, farewell sweete Ladie.
Exeunt Bennolio, Mercurio.
Nurs:

of Romeo and Iuliet.

Nur: Marry farewell. Pray what saucie merchant was this that was so full of his roperipe?

Rom: A gentleman Nurse that loues to heare himselfe talke, and will speake more in an houre than hee will stand to in a month.

Nur: If hee stand to anie thing against mee, I'e take him downe if he were lustier than he is: if I cannot take him downe, Ile finde them that shall: I am none of his flurt-gills, I am none of his skaines mates.

She turnes to Peter her man.

And thou like a knaue must stand by, and see euerie Iacke vse me at his pleasure.

Pet: I see no bodie vse you at his pleasure, if I had, I would soone haue drawen: you know my toole is as soone out as anothers if I see time and place.

Nur: Now afore God he hath so vext me, that euerie member about me quiuers: scuruie Iacke. But as I said, my Ladie bad me seeke ye out, and what shee bad me tell yee, that Ile keepe to my selfe: but if you should lead her into a fooles paradice as they saye, it were a verie grosse kinde of behauiour as they say, for the Gentlewoman is yong. Now if you should deale doubly with her, it were verie weake dealing, and not to be offered to anie Gentlewoman.

Rom: Nurse, commend me to thy Ladie, tell her I protest.

Nur: Good heart: yfaith Ile tell her so: oh she will be a ioyfull woman.

Rom: Why, what wilt thou tell her?

Nur: That you doo protest: which (as I take it) is a Gentlemanlike proffer.

Rom: Bid her get leaue to morrow morning
To come to shrift to Frier *Laurence* cell:
And stay thou Nurse behinde the Abbey wall,
My man shall come to thee, and bring along
The cordes, made like a tackled staire,
Which to the high top-gallant of my ioy

E 3   Must

The excellent Tragedie

Must be my conduct in the secret night.
Hold, take that for thy paines.
   Nur: No, not a penie truly.
   Rom: I say you shall not chuse.
   Nur: Well, to morrow morning she shall not faile.
   Rom: Farewell, be trustie, and Ile quite thy paine. *Exit*
   Nur: Peter, take my fanne, and goe before. *Ex.omnes.*

              Enter Iuliet.

   Iul: The clocke stroke nine when I did send my Nurse
In halfe an houre she promist to returne.
Perhaps she cannot finde him. Thats not so,
Oh she is lazie, Loues heralds should be thoughts,
And runne more swift, than hastie powder fierd,
Doth hurrie from the fearfull Cannons mouth.
              Enter Nurse.
Oh now she comes. Tell me gentle Nurse,
What sayes my Loue?
   Nur: Oh I am wearie, let mee rest a while. Lord how
my bones ake. Oh wheres my man? Giue me some aqua
vitæ.
   Iul: I would thou hadst my bones, and I thy newes,
   Nur: Fie, what a iaunt haue I had: and my backe a to-
ther side. Lord, Lord, what a case am I in,
   Iul: But tell me sweet Nurse, what sayes Romeo?
   Nur: Romeo, nay, alas you cannot chuse a man. Hees
no bodie, he is not the Flower of curtesie, he is not a proper
man: and for a hand, and a foote, and a baudie, wel go thy
way wench, thou hast it ifaith. Lord, Lord, how my head
beates?
   Iul: What of all this? tell me what sayes he to our mariage?
   Nur: Marry he sayes like an honest Gentleman, and a
kinde, and I warrant a vertuous: wheres your Mother?
   Iul: Lord, Lord, how odly thou repliest? He saies like a
                                                   kinde

of Romeo and Iuliet.

kinde Gentleman, and an honest, and a vertuous; wheres your mother?

Nur: Marry come vp, cannot you stay a while? is this the poultesse for mine aking boanes? next arrant youl haue done, euen doot your selfe.

Iul: Nay stay sweet Nurse, I doo intreate thee now, What sayes my Loue, my Lord, my *Romeo*?

Nur: Goe, hye you straight to Friar *Laurence* Cell, And frame a scuse that you must goe to shrift: There stayes a Bridegroome to make you a Bride. Now comes the wanton blood vp in your cheekes, I must prouide a ladder made of cordes, With which your Lord must clime a birdes nest soone. I must take paines to further your delight, But you must beare the burden soone at night. Doth this newes please you now?

Iul: How doth her latter words reuiue my hart. Thankes gentle Nurse, dispatch thy busines, And Ile not faile to meete my *Romeo*.   *Exeunt.*

Enter Romeo, Frier.

Rom: Now Father *Laurence*, in thy holy grant Consists the good of me and *Iuliet*.

Fr: Without more words I will doo all I may, To make you happie if in me it lye.

Rom: This morning here she pointed we should meet, And consumate those neuer parting bands, Witnes of our harts loue by ioyning hands, And come she will.

Fr: I gesse she will indeed, Youths loue is quicke, swifter than swiftest speed.

Enter Iuliet somewhat fast, and embraceth Romeo.

See where she comes. So light of foote nere hurts the troden flower: Of loue and ioy, see see the soueraigne power.

Iul: *Romeo*.

Rom:

37

The excellent Tragedie

Rom: My *Iuliet* welcome. As doo waking eyes
(Cloa'sd in Nights mysts) attend the frolicke Day,
So *Romeo* hath expected *Iuliet*,
And thou art come.

Iul: I am (if I be Day)
Come to my Sunne: shine foorth, and make me faire.

Rom: All beauteous fairnes dwelleth in thine eyes.

Iul: *Romeo* from thine all brightnes doth arise.

Fr: Come wantons, come, the stealing houres do passe
Defer imbracements till some fitter time,
Part for a while, you shall not be alone,
Till holy Church haue ioynd ye both in one.

Rom: Lead holy Father, all delay seemes long.

Iul: Make hast, make hast, this lingring doth vs wrong.

Fr: O, soft and faire makes sweetest worke they say.
Hast is a common hindrer in crosse way.   *Exeunt omnes.*

Enter *Benuolio, Mercutio.*

Ben: I pree thee good *Mercutio* lets retire,
The day is hot, the *Capels* are abroad.

Mer: Thou art like one of those, that when hee comes
into the confines of a tauerne, claps me his rapier on the
boord, and sayes, God send me no need of thee: and by
the operation of the next cup of wine, he drawes it on the
drawer, when indeed there is no need.

Ben: Am I like such a one?

Mer: Go too, thou art as hot a Iacke being mooude,
and as soone mooude to be moodie, and as soone moodie to
be mooud.

Ben: And what too?

Mer: Nay, and there were two such, wee should haue
none shortly. Didst not thou fall out with a man for crack-
ing of nuts, hauing no other reason, but because thou hadst
hasill eyes? what eye but such an eye would haue pickt out
such a quarrell? With another for coughing, because hee
wakd

of Romeo and Iuliet.

wakd thy dogge that laye a sleepe in the Sunne? With a
Taylor for wearing his new dublet before Easter: and
with another for tying his new shoes with olde ribands.
And yet thou wilt forbid me of quarrelling.

Ben: By my head heere comes a *Capulet*.

Enter Tybalt.

Mer: By my heele I care not.

Tyb: Gentlemen a word with one of you.

Mer: But one word with one of vs? You had best couple
it with somewhat, and make it a word and a blow.

Tyb: I am apt enough to that if I haue occasion.

Mer: Could you not take occasion?

Tyb: *Mercutio* thou consorts with *Romeo*?

Mer: Consort. Zwounes consort: the slaue wil make fidlers of vs. If you doe sirs, look for nothing but discord: For
heeres my fiddle-sticke.

Enter Romeo.

Tyb: Well peace be with you, heere comes my man.

Mer: But Ile be hanged if he weare your lyuery: Mary
go before into the field, and he may be your follower, so in
that sence your worship may call him man.

Tyb: Romeo the hate I beare to thee can affoord no better word then these, thou art a villaine.

Rom: Tybalt the loue I beare to thee, doth excuse the
appertaining rage to such a word: villaine am I none, ther-
fore I well perceiue thou knowst me not.

Tyb: Bace boy this cannot serue thy turne, and therefore
drawe.

Ro: I doe protest I neuer iniured thee, but loue thee better than thou canst deuise, till thou shalt know the reason of
my loue.

Mer: O dishonorable vile submission. *Allastockado* caries
it away. You Ratcatcher, come backe, come backe.

Tyb: What wouldest with me?

E   *Mer:*

The excellent Tragedie

Mer: Nothing King of Cates, but borrow one of your nine liues, therefore come drawe your rapier out of your scabard, least mine be about your eares ere you be aware.

Rom: Stay *Tibalt*, hould *Mercutio: Benuolio* beate downe their weapons.

Tibalt vnder Romeos armes thrusts Mer-
cutio, in and flyes.

Mer: Is he gone, hath hee nothing? A poxe on your houses.

Rom: What art thou hurt man, the wound is not deepe.

Mer: Noe nor so deepe as a Well, nor so wide as a barne doore, but it will serue I warrant. What meant you to come betweene vs? I was hurt vnder your arme.

Rom: I did all for the best.

Mer: A poxe of your houses, I am fairely drest. Sirra goe fetch me a Surgeon.

Boy: I goe my Lord.

Mer: I am peppered for this world, I am sped yfaith, he hath made wormes meate of me, & ye aske for me to-morrow you shall finde me a graue-man. A poxe of your houses, I shall be fairely mounted vpon foure mens shoulders: For your house of the *Mountegues* and the *Capolets:* and then some peasantly rogue, some Sexton, some base slaue shall write my Epitaph, that *Tybalt* came and broke the Princes Lawes, and *Mercutio* was slaine for the first and second cause. Wher's the Surgeon?

Boy: Hee's come sir.

Mer: Now heele keepe a mumbling in my guts on the other side, come *Benuolio*, lend me thy hand: a poxe of your houses. *Exeunt*

Rom: This Gentleman the Princes neere Alie, My very frend hath tane this mortall wound In my behalfe, my reputation staind With *Tibalts* slaunder, *Tybalt* that an houre Hath beene my kinsman, Ah *Iuliet*

Thy

of Romeo and Iuliet.

Thy beautie makes me thus effeminate,
And in my temper softens valors steele.

Enter Benuolio.

Ben: Ah *Romeo Romeo* braue *Mercutio* is dead,
That gallant spirit hath a spir'd the cloudes,
Which too vntimely scorn'd the lowly earth.
  Rom: This daies black fate, on more daies doth depend
This but begins what other dayes must end.

Enter Tibalt.

Ben: Heere comes the furious *Tibalt* backe againe,
  Rom: A liue in tryumph and *Mercutio* slaine?
Away to heauen respectiue lenity:
And fier eyed fury be my conduct now.
Now *Tibalt* take the villaine backe againe,
Which late thou gau'st me: for *Mercutios* soule,
Is but a little way aboue the cloudes,
And staies for thine to beare him company.
Or thou, or I, or both shall follow him.

Fight, Tibalt falles.

Ben: *Romeo* away, thou seest that *Tibalt's* slaine,
The Citizens approach, away, be gone
Thou wilt be taken.
  Rom: Ah I am fortunes slaue.

Exeunt

Enter Citizens.

Watch. Wher's he that slue *Mercutio*, *Tybalt* that villaine?
  Ben: There is that *Tybalt*.

F 2 *Watch:* Vp

The excellent Tragedie

1581	Vp sirra goe with vs.
1583-4	*Enter Prince, Cipolets wife.*
1585	*Pry:* Where be the vile beginners of this fray?
	Ben: Ah Noble Prince I can discouer all
	The most vnlucky mannage of this brawle,
	Heere lyes the man slaine by yong *Romeo*,
	That slew thy kinsman braue *Mercutio*.
1590	*M:* Tiball, Tyball, O my brothers child,
	Vnhappie sight? Ah the blood is spilt
	Of my deare kinsman, Prince as thou art true:
1593	For blood of ours, shed bloud of *Mountagew*.
1595	*Pry:* Speake *Benuolio* who began this fray?
	Ben: Tibalt heere slaine whom *Romeos* hand did slay.
	Romeo who spake him fayre bid him bethinke
1598	How nice the quarrell was,
1598+	But *Tibalt* still persisting in his wrong,
	The stout *Mercutio* drewe to calme the storme,
1608-9	Which *Romeo* seeing cal'd stay Gentlemen,
1609+	And on me cry'd, who drew to part their strife,
1610	And with his agill arme yong *Romeo*,
1610+	As fast as tung cryde peace, sought peace to make.
	While they were enterchanging thrusts and blows,
1611	Vnder yong *Romeos* laboring arme to part,
1612	The furious *Tybalt* cast an enuious thrust,
1612-13	That rid the life of stout *Mercutio*.
1613-14	With that he fled, but presently return'd,
1614+	And with his rapier braued *Romeo*.
1615	That had but newly enterrain'd reuenge.
1616-17	And ere I could draw forth my rapyer
1617	To part their furie, downe did *Tybalt* fall,
1618	And this way *Romeo* fled.
1620-1	*Mo:* He is a *Mountagew* and speakes partiall,
	Some twentie of them fought in this blacke strife:
1622	And all those twenty could but kill one life.

1230
1240
1250

I doe

42

of Romeo and Iuliet.

I doo intreate sweete Prince thou't iustice giue,
Romeo slew *Tybalt*, *Romeo* may not liue.
   Prin: And for that offence
Immediately we doo exile him hence.
I haue an interest in your hates proceeding,
My blood for your rude braules doth lye a bleeding,
But Ile amerce you with so large a fine,
That you shall all repent the losse of mine.
I will be deafe to pleading and excuses,
Nor teares nor prayers shall purchase for abuses.
Pittie shall dwell and gouerne with vs still:
Mercie to all but murdrers, pardoning none that kill.
                         Exeunt omnes.

         Enter Iuliet.

   Iul: Gallop apace you fierie footed steedes
To *Phœbus* mansion, such a Waggoner
As *Phaeton*, would quickly bring you thether,
And send in cloudie night immediately.

   *Enter Nurse wringing her hands, with the ladder
         of cordes in her lap.*
But how now Nurse: O Lord, why lookst thou sad?
What hast thou there, the cordes?
   Nur: I, I, the cordes: alacke we are vndone,
We are vndone, Ladie we are vndone.
   Iul: What diuell art thou that torments me thus?
   Nurs: Alack the day, hees dead, hees dead, hees dead.
   Iul: This torture should be roard in dismall hell.
Can heauens be so enuious?
   Nur: *Romeo* can if heauens cannot.
I saw the wound, I saw it with mine eyes,
God saue the sample, on his manly breast:
A bloodie coarse, a piteous bloodie coarse,
All pale as ashes, I swouned at the sight.
       F 3   *Iul*:

The excellent Tragedie

Iul: Ah *Romeo, Romeo,* what disaster hap
Hath seuerd thee from thy true *Iuliet* ?
Ah why shou'd Heauen so much conspire with Woe,
Or Fate giuue our happie Marriage,
So soone to sunder vs by timelesse Death ?

Nur: O *Tybalt, Tybalt,* the best frend I had,
O honest *Tybalt,* curteous Gentleman.

Iul: What storme is this that blowes so contrarie,
Is *Tybalt* dead, and *Romeo* murdered :
My deare loude cousen, and my dearest Lord.
Then let the trumpet sound a generall doome,
These two being dead, then liuing is there none.

Nur: *Tybalt* is dead, and *Romeo* banished,
Romeo that murdred him is banished.

Iul: Ah heauens, did *Romeos* hand shed *Tybalts* blood?

Nur: It did, it did, alacke the day it did.

Iul: O serpents hate, hid with a flowring face :
O painted sepulcher, including filth.
Was neuer booke containing so foule matter,
So fairly bound. Ah, what meant *Romeo* ?

Nur: There is no truth, no faith, no honestie in men :
All false, all faithles, periurde, all forsworne.
Shame come to *Romeo.*

Iul: A blister on that tung, he was not borne to shame :
Vpon his face Shame is ashamyde to sit.
But wherefore villaine didst thou kill my Cousen ?
That villaine Cousen would haue kild my husband.
All this is comfort. But there yet remaines
VVorse than his death, which faine I would forget :
But ah, it presseth to my memorie,
Romeo is banished. Ah that word, Banished.
Is worse than death, *Romeo* is banished,
Is Father, Mother, *Tybalt, Iuliet,*
All kill'd, all slaine, all dead, all banished.
Where are my Father and my Mother Nurse ?

Nur: VVeeping and wayling ouer *Tybalts* coarse.

VVill

of Romeo and Iuliet.

VVill you goe to them?

Iul: I, I, when theirs are spent,
Mine shall be shed for *Romeos* banishment.

Nur: Ladie, your *Romeo* will be here to night,
Ile to him, he is hid at *Lawrence* Cell.

Iul: Doo so, and beare this Ring to my true Knight,
And bid him come to take his last farewell.   *Exeunt.*

Enter Frier.

Fr: Romeo come forth, come forth thou fearfull man,
Affliction is enamourd on thy parts,
And thou art wedded to Calamitie.

Enter Romeo.

Rom: Father what newes, what is the Princes doome,
VVhat sorrow craues acquaintance at our hands,
VVhich yet we know not.

Fr: Too familiar
Is my yong sonne with such sowre companie:
I bring thee tidings of the Princes doome.

Rom: VVhat lesse than doomes day is the Princes doome?

Fr: A gentler iudgement vanisht from his lips,
Not bodies death, but bodies banishment.

Rom: Ha, Banished? be mercifull, say death:
For Exile hath more terror in his lookes,
Than death it selfe, doo not say Banishment.

Fr: Hence from *Verona* art thou banished?
Be patient, for the world is broad and wide.

Rom: There is no world without *Verona* walls,
But purgatorie, torture, hell it selfe,
Hence banished, is banisht from the world:
And world exilde is death. Calling death banishment,
Thou cutst my head off with a golden axe,
And smilest vpon the stroke that murders me.

Fr: Oh monstrous sinne, O rude vnthankfulnes:
Thy fault our law calls death, but the milde Prince
(Taking thy part) hath rusht aside the law,

And

45

The excellent Tragedie

And turnd that blacke word death to banishment:
This is meere mercie, and thou seest it not.
   Rom: Tis torture and not mercie, heauen is heere
Where *Iuliet* liues: and euerie cat and dog,
And little mouse, euerie vnworthie thing
Liue here in heauen, and may looke on her,
But *Romeo* may not. More validitie,
More honourable state, more courtship liues
In carrion flyes, than *Romeo*: they may seaze
On the white wonder of faire *Iuliets* skinne,
And steale immortall kisses from her lips:
But *Romeo* may not, he is banished.
Flies may doo this, but I from this must flye.
Oh Father, hadst thou no strong poyson mixt,
No sharpe ground knife, no present meane of death,
Though nere so meane, but banishment
To torture me withall: ah, banished.
O Frier, the damned vse that word in hell:
Howling attends it. How hadst thou the heart,
Being a Diuine, a ghostly Confessor,
A sinne absoluer, and my frend profest,
To mangle me with that word, Banishment?
  Fr: Thou fond mad man, heare me but speake a word,
  Rom: O, thou wilt talke againe of banishment.
  Fr: Ile giue thee armour to beare off this word,
Aduersities sweete milke, philosophie,
To comfort thee though thou be banished.
  Rom: Yet Banished? hang vp philosophie,
Vnlesse philosophie can make a *Iuliet*,
Displant a Towne, reuerse a Princes doome,
It helpes not, it preuailes not, talke no more.
  Fr: O, now I see that mad men haue no eares.
  Rom: How should they, when that wise men haue no eyes.
  Fr: Let me dispute with thee of thy estate.
  Rom: Thou canst not speak of what thou dost not feele.

Wert

of Romeo and Iuliet.

Wert thou as young as I, *Iuliet* thy Loue,
An houre but married, *Tybalt* murdred,
Doting like me, and like me banished,
Then mightst thou speake, then mightst thou teare thy
    hayre,
And fall vpon the ground as I doe now,
Taking the measure of an vnmade graue.

              Nurse knockes.

  Fr: Romeo arise, stand vp thou wilt be taken,
I heare one knocke, arise and get thee gone.
  Nu: Hoe Fryer.
  Fr: Gods will what wilfulnes is this?

              Shee knockes againe.

  Nur: Hoe Fryer open the doore.
  Fr: By and by I come. Who is there?
  Nur: One from Lady *Iuliet.*
  Fr: Then come neare.
  Nur: Oh holy Fryer, tell mee oh holy Fryer,
Where is my Ladies Lord? Wher's *Romeo?*
  Fr: There on the ground, with his owne teares made
drunke.
  Nur: Oh he is euen in my Mistresse case.
Iust in her case. Oh wofull simpathy,
Pitteous predicament, euen so lyes shee,
Weeping and blubbring, blubbring and weeping:
Stand vp, stand vp, stand and you be a man,
For *Iuliets* sake, for her sake rise and stand,
Why should you fall into so deep an O.

              He rises.

  Romeo: Nurse.
  Nur: Ah sir, ah sir, Wel death's the end of all.

              G   Rom

The excellent Tragedie

Rom: Spakest thou of *Iuliet*, how is it with her?
Doth she not thinke me an olde murderer,
Now I haue stainde the childhood of her ioy,
With bloud remou'd but little from her owne?
Where is she? and how doth she? And what sayes
My conceal'd Lady to our canceld loue?

  Nur: Oh she saith nothing, but weepes and pules,
And now fals on her bed, now on the ground,
And *Tybalt* cryes, and then on *Romeo* calles.

  Rom: As if that name shot from the deadly leuel of a gun
Did murder her, as that names cursed hand
Murderd her kinsman. Ah tell me holy Fryer
In what vile part of this Anatomy
Doth my name lye? Tell me that I may sacke
The hatefull mansion?

        He offers to stab himselfe, and Nurse snatches
                the dagger away.

  Nur: Ah?
  Fri Hold, stay thy hand: art thou a man? thy forme
Cryes out thou art, but thy wilde actes denote
The vnreasonable furyes of a beast.
Vnseemely woman in a seeming man,
Or ill beseeming beast in seeming both,
Thou hast amaz'd me. By my holy order,
I thought thy disposition better temperd,
Hast thou slaine *Tybalt*? wilt thou slay thy selfe?
And slay thy Lady too, that liues in thee?
Rouse vp thy spirits, thy Lady *Iuliet* liues,
For whose sweet sake thou wert but lately dead:
There art thou happy. *Tybalt* would kill thee,
But thou sluest *Tybalt*, there art thou happy too.
A packe of blessings lights vpon thy backe,
Happines Courts thee in his best array:
But like a misbehaude and sullen wench
Thou frownst vpon thy Fate that smilles on thee,
                                                    Take

of Romeo and Iulet.

Take heede, take heede, for such dye miserable,
Goe get thee to thy loue as was decreed:
Ascend her Chamber Window, hence and comfort her,
But looke thou stay not till the watch be set,
For then thou canst not passe to *Mantua.*
Nurse prouide all things in a readines,
Comfort thy Mistresse, haste the house to bed,
Which heauy sorrow makes them apt vnto.

   Nur: Good Lord what a thing learning is,
I could haue stayde heere all this night
To heare good counsell. Well Sir,
Ile tell my Lady that you will come.
   Rom: Doe so and bidde my sweet prepare to childe,
Farwell good Nurse.

   Nurse offers to goe in and turnes againe.

   Nur: Heere is a Ring Sir, that she bad me giue you,
   Rom: How well my comfort is reuiud by this.

                                         Exit Nurse.

   Fr: Soiorne in *Mantua,* Ile finde out your man,
And he shall signifie from time to time:
Euery good hap that doth befall thee heere,
Farwell.
   Rom: But that a ioy, past ioy cryes out on me,
It were a griefe so breefe to part with thee.

   Enter olde Capolet and his wife, with
          County Paris.

   Cap: Thinges haue fallen out Sir so vnluck'ly,
That we haue had no time to moue my daughter.

The excellent Tragedie

Looke yee Sir, she lou'd her kinsman dearly,
And so did I. Well, we were borne to dye.
Wife w'her's your daughter, is she in her chamber?
I thinke she meanes not to come downe to night.

 Par: These times of woe affoord no time to wooe,
Maddam farwell, commend me to your daughter.

*Paris offers to goe in, and Capolet
calles him againe.*

 Cap: Sir Paris, Ile make a desperate tender of my child,
I thinke she will be rulde in all respectes by mee:
But soft, what day is this?

 Par: Munday my Lord.

 Cap: Oh then Wensday is too soone,
On Thursday let it be: you shall be maried.
Wee'le make no great a doe, a frend or two, or so:
For looke ye Sir, Tybalt being slaine so lately,
It will be thought we held him carelesly:
If we should reuell much, therefore we will haue
Some halfe a dozen frends and make no more adoe.
But what say you to Thursday.

 Par: My Lorde I wishe that Thursday were to morrow.

 Cap: Wife goe you to your daughter, ere you goe to
bed,
Acquaint her with the County Paris loue,
Fare well my Lord till Thursday next.
Wife gette you to your daughter, Light to my Chamber.
Afore me it is so very very late,
That we may call it earely by and by.
                                      Exeunt.

Enter

50

of Romeo and Iuliet.

Enter Romeo and Iuliet at the window.

Iul: Wilt thou be gone? It is not yet nere day,
It was the Nightingale and not the Larke
That pierst the fearfull hollow of thine eare:
Nightly she sings on yon Pomegranate tree,
Beleeue me loue, it was the Nightingale.

Rom: It was the Larke, the Herald of the Morne,
And not the Nightingale. See Loue what enuious strakes
Doo lace the seuering clowdes in yonder East.
Nights candles are burnt out, and iocond Day
Stands tiptoes on the myftie mountaine tops.
I must be gone and liue, or stay and dye.

Iul: Yon light is not day light, I know it I:
It is some Meteor that the Sunne exhales,
To be this night to thee a Torch-bearer,
And light thee on thy way to *Mantua*.
Then stay awhile, thou shalt not goe soone.

Rom: Let me stay here, let me be tane, and dye:
If thou wilt haue it so, I am content.
Ile say yon gray is not the Mornings Eye,
It is the pale reflex of *Cynthias* brow.
Ile say it is the Nightingale that beates
The vaultie heauen so high aboue our heads,
And not the Larke the Messenger of Morne.
Come death and welcome, *Iuliet* wils it so.
What sayes my Loue? lets talke, tis not yet day.

Iuli: It is, it is, be gone, flye hence away.
It is the Larke that sings so out of tune,
Straining harsh Discords and vnpleasing Sharpes.
Some say, the Larke makes sweete Diuision:

G 3   Thia

The excellent Tragedie

This doth not so: for this diuideth vs.
Some say the Larke and loathed Toad change eyes,
I would that now they had changd voyces too:
Since arme from arme her voyce doth vs affray,
Hunting thee hence with Huntsvp to the day,
So now be gone, more light and light it growes.

   Rom: More light and light, more darke and darke our
            woes.
Farewell my Loue, one kisse and Ile descend.

He goeth downe.

   Jul: Art thou gone so, my Lord, my Loue, my Frend?
I must heare from thee euerie day in the hower:
For in an hower there are manie minutes,
Minutes are dayes, so will I number them:
Oh, by this count I shall be much in yeares,
Ere I see thee againe.
   Rom: Farewell, I will omit no opportunitie
That may conueigh my greetings loue to thee.
   Jul: Oh, thinkst thou we shall euer meete againe.
   Rom: No doubt, no doubt, and all this woe shall serue
For sweete discourses in the time to come.
   Jul: Oh God, I haue an ill diuining soule,
Me thinkes I see thee now thou art below
Like one dead in the bottome of a Tombe:
Either mine ey-sight failes, or thou lookst pale.
   Rom: And trust me Loue, in my eye so doo you,
Drie sorrow drinkes our blood: adieu, adieu.   *Exit.*

Enter Nurse hastely.

   Nyr: Madame beware, take heed the day is broke,
Your Mother's comming to your Chamber, make all sure.
         She goeth downe from the window.

                                              Enter

of Romeo and Iuliet.

Enter Iuliets Mother, Nurse.

Moth: Where are you Daughter?
Nur: What Ladie, Lambe, what *Iuliet*?
Iul: How now, who calls?
Nur: It is your Mother.
Moth: Why how now *Iuliet*?
Iul: Madam, I am not well.
Moth: What euermore weeping for your Cosens death?
I thinke thoult wash him from his graue with teares.
Iul: I cannot chuse, hauing so great a losse.
Moth: I cannot blame thee.
But it greeues thee more that Villaine liues.
Iul: What Villaine Madame?
Moth: That Villaine *Romeo*.
Iul: Villaine and he are manie miles a sunder.
Moth: Content thee Girle, if I could finde a man
I soone would send to *Mantua* where he is,
That should bestow on him so sure a draught,
As he should soone beare *Tybalt* companie.
Iul: Finde you the meanes, and Ile finde such a man:
For whilest he liues, my heart shall nere be light
Till I behold him, dead is my poore heart.
Thus for a Kinsman vext?   (newes?
Moth: Well let that passe. I come to bring thee ioyfull
Iul: And ioy comes well in such a needfull time.
Moth: Well then, thou hast a carefull Father Girle,
And one who pittying thy needfull state,
Hath found thee out a happie day of ioy.
Iul: What day is that I pray you?
Moth: Marry my Childe,
                                                    The

The excellent Tragedie

The gallant, yong and youthfull Gentleman,
The Countie *Paris* at Saint *Peters* Church,
Early next Thursday morning must prouide,
To make you there a glad and ioyfull Bride.
  Iul: Now by Saint *Peters* Church and *Peter* too,
He shall not there make mee a ioyfull Bride.
Are these the newes you had to tell me of?
Marrie here are newes indeed. Madame I will not marrie
                yet,
And when I doo, it shalbe rather *Romeo* whom I hate,
Than Countie *Paris* that I cannot loue.

             Enter olde Capolet.

  Moth: Here comes your Father, you may tell him so.
  Capo: Why how now, euermore showring?
In one little bodie thou resemblest a sea, a barke, a storme:
For this thy bodie which I tearme a barke,
Still floating in thy euerfalling teares,
And tost with sighes arising from thy hart:
Will without succour shipwracke presently.
But heare you Wife, what haue you sounded her, what sees
                she to it?
  Moth: I haue, but she will none she thankes ye:
VVould God that she were married to her graue.
  Capo: What will shee not, doth she not thanke vs, doth
she not wexe proud?
  Iul: Not proud ye haue, but thankfull that ye haue:
Proud can I neuer be of that I hate,
But thankfull euen for hate that is ment loue.
  Capo: Proud and I thanke you, and I thanke you not,
And yet not proud. VVhats here, chop logicke,
Proud me no prouds, nor thanke me no thankes,
But settle your fine ioynts on Thursday next
To goe with *Paris* to Saint *Peters* Church,
Or I will drag you on a hurdle thether.
                                            Out

of Romeo and Iuliet.

Out you greene sicknes baggage, out you tallow face.
  Iu: Good father heare me speake?

She kneeles downe.
  Cap: I tell thee what, eyther resolue on thursday next
To goe with *Paris* to Saint Peters Church:
Or henceforth neuer looke me in the face,
Speake not, reply not, for my fingers ytch,
Why wife, we thought that we were scarcely blest
That God had sent vs but this onely chyld:
But now I see this one is one too much,
And that we haue a crosse in hauing her.
  Nur: Mary God in heauen blesse her my Lord,
You are too blame to rate her so.
  Cap. And why my Lady wisedome: hold your tung,
Good prudence: smatter with your gossips, goe.
  Nur: Why my Lord I speake no treason.
  Cap: Oh goddegodden.
Vtter your grauity ouer a gossips boule,
For heere we need it not.
  Mo: My Lord ye are too hotte.
  Cap: Gods blessed mother wife it mads me,
Day, night, early, late, at home, abroad,
Alone, in company, waking or sleeping,
Still my care hath beene to see her matcht,
And hauing now found out a Gentleman,
Of Princely parentage, youthfull, and nobly trainde,
Stuft as they say with honorable parts,
Proportioned as ones heart coulde wish a man:
And then to haue a wretched whyning foole,
A puling mammet in her fortunes tender,
To say I cannot loue, I am too young, I pray you pardon
   mee?
But if you cannot wedde Ile pardon you,
Graze where you will, you shall not house with me,
Looke to it, thinke ont, I doe not vse to iest.

H   I

The excellent Tragedie

I tell yee what, Thursday is neere,
Lay hand on heart, aduise, bethinke your selfe,
If you be mine, Ile giue you to my frend:
If not, hang, drowne, starue, beg,
Dye in the streetes, for by my Soule
Ile neuer more acknowledge thee,
Nor what I haue shall euer doe thee good,
Thinke ont, looke toot, I doe not vse to iest. *Exit.*

Iuli. Is there no pitty hanging in the cloudes,
That lookes into the bottom of my woes?
I doe beseech you Madame, cast me not away,
Defer this mariage for a day or two,
Or if you cannot, make my mariage bed
In that dimme monument where *Tybalt* lyes.

Moth. Nay be assured I will not speake a word,
Do what thou wilt for I haue done with thee. *Exit.*

Iul. Ah Nurse, what comfort? what counsell canst thou
giue me.

Nur. Now trust me Madame, I know not what to say,
Your *Romeo* he is banisht, and all the world to nothing
He neuer dares returne to challendge you,
Now I thinke good you marry with this County,
Oh he is a gallant Gentleman, *Romeo* is but a dishclout
In respect of him, I promise you
I thinke you happy in this second match,
As for your husband he is dead,
Or twere as good he were, for you haue no vse of him.

Iul. Speakst thou this from thy heart?

Nur. I and from my soule, or els beshrew them both.

Iul. Amen.

Nur. What say you Madame?

Iul. Well, thou hast comforted me wondrous much,
I pray thee goe thy waies vnto my mother
Tell her I am gone hauing displeasde my Father,
To Fryer *Laurence* Cell to confesse me,
And to be absolu'd.

of Romeo and Iuliet.

Nurs: I will, and this is wisely done.
She lookes after Nurse.

Iuli Auncient damnation, O most cursed fiend.
Is it more sinne to wish me thus forsworne,
Or to dispraise him with the selfe same tongue
That thou hast praisde him with aboue compare
So many thousand times? Goe Counsellor,
Thou and my bosom henceforth shel be twaine.
Ile to the Fryer to know his remedy,
If all faile els, I haue the power to dye.
Exit.

Enter Fryer and Paris.

Fr: On Thursday say ye: the time is very short,
Par: My Father *Capolet* will haue it so,
And I am nothing slacke to slow his hast.
Fri You say you doe not know the Ladies minde?
Vneuen is the course, I like it not.
Par: Immoderately she weepes for *Tybalts* death,
And therefore haue I little talkt of loue,
For *Venus* smiles not in a house of teares,
Now Sir, her father thinkes it daungerous;
That she doth giue her sorrow so much sway.
And in his wisedome hasts our mariage,
To stop the inundation of her teares,
Which too much minded by her selfe alone
May be put from her by societie.
Now doe ye know the reason of this hast,
Fr: I would I knew not why it should be slowd.
H 2   *Enter*

The excellent Tragedie

Enter Paris.

Heere comes the Lady to my cell.
   Par: Welcome my loue, my Lady and my wife:
   Iu: That may be sir, when I may be a wife,
   Par: That may be, must be loue, on thursday next.
   Iu: What must be shalbe.
   Fr: Thats a certaine text.
   Par: What come ye to confession to this Fryer.
   Iu: To tell you that were to confesse to you.
   Par: Do not deny to him that you loue me.
   Iuh I will confesse to you that I loue him,
   Par: So I am sure you will that you loue me,
   Iu: And if I doe, it wilbe of more price,
Being spoke behinde your backe, than to your face.
   Par: Poore soule thy face is much abus'd with teares.
   Iu: The teares haue got small victory by that,
For it was bad enough before their spite.
   Par: Thou wrongst it more than teares by that report.
   Iu: That is no wrong sir, that is a truth;
And what I spake I spake it to my face.
   Par: Thy face is mine and thou hast slaundred it.
   Iu: It may be so, for it is not mine owne.
Are you at leasure holy Father now:
Or shall I come to you at euening Masse?
   Fr: My leasure serues me pensiue daughter now.
My Lord we must entreate the time alone.
   Par: God sheild I should disturbe deuotion,
Iuliet farewell, and keep this holy kisse.
                                    Exit Paris.

   Iu: Goe shut the doore and when thou hast done so,
Come weepe with me that am past cure, past help.
   Fr: Ah *Iuliet* I already know thy griefe,
I heare thou must and nothing may proroge it,

                                               On

of Romeo and Iuliet.

On Thursday next be married to the Countie,
   Iul: Tell me not Frier that thou hearst of it,
Vnlesse thou tell me how we may preuent it.
Giue me some sudden counsell: els behold
Twixt my extreames and me, this bloodie Knife
Shall play the Vmpeere, arbitrating that
Which the Commission of thy yeares and arte
Could to no issue of true honour bring.
Speake not, be briefe: for I desire to die,
If what thou speakst, speake not of remedie.
   Fr: Stay *Iuliet*, I doo spie a kinde of hope,
VVhich craues as desperate an execution,
As that is desperate we would preuent.
If rather than to marrie Countie *Paris*
Thou hast the strength or will to slay thy selfe,
Tis not vnlike that thou wilt vndertake
A thing like death to chyde away this shame,
That coapst with death it selfe to flye from blame.
And if thou doost, Ile giue thee remedie.
   Iul: Oh bid me leape (rather than marrie *Paris*)
From off the battlements of yonder tower:
Or chaine me to some steepie mountaines top,
VVhere roaring Beares and sauage Lions are:
Or shut me nightly in a Charnell-house,
VVith reekie shankes, and yeolow chaples sculls:
Or lay me in tombe with one new dead:
Things that to heare them namde haue made me tremble;
And I will doo it without feare or doubt,
To keep my selfe a faithfull vnstaind VVife
To my deere Lord, my deerest *Romeo.*
   Fr: Hold *Iuliet*, hie thee home, get thee to bed,
Let not thy Nurse lye with thee in thy Chamber:
And when thou art alone, take thou this Violl,
And this distilled Liquor drinke thou off:
VVhen presently through all thy veynes shall run
A dull and heauie slumber, which shall seaze

The excellent Tragedie

Each vitall spirit: for no Pulse shall keepe
His naturall progresse, but surcease to beate:
No signe of breath shall testifie thou liust,
And in this borrowed likenes of shrunke death,
Thou shalt remaine full two and fortie houres.
And when thou art laid in thy Kindreds Vault,
Ile send in hast to *Mantua* to thy Lord,
And he shall come and take thee from thy graue.
    Iul: Frier I goe, be sure thou send for my deare *Romeo.*
                                    Exeunt.

Enter olde Capolet, his Wife, Nurse, and
Seruingman.

  Capo: Where are you sirra?
  Ser: Heere forsooth.
  Capo: Goe, prouide me twentie cunning Cookes.
  Ser: I warrant you Sir, let me alone for that, Ile knowe
them by licking their fingers.
  Capo: How canst thou know them so?
  Ser: Ah Sir, tis an ill Cooke cannot licke his owne fingers.
  Capo: Well get you gone.

Exit Seruingman.

But wheres this Head-strong?
  Moth: Shees gone (my Lord) to Frier *Laurence* Cell
To be confest.
  Capo: Ah, he may hap to doo some good of her,
A headstrong selfewild harlotrie it is.

                                    Enter

of Romeo and Iuliet.

Enter Iuliet.

Moth: See here she commeth from Confession. 2439
Capo: How now my Head-strong, where haue you bin 2441-2
gadding? 2442
Iul: Where I haue learned to repent the sin
Of froward wilfull opposition
Gainst you and your behests, and am enioynd
By holy *Laurence* to fall prostrate here,
And craue remission of so soule a fact. 2447

She kneeles downe. 2447+

Moth: Why thats well said. 2454
Capo: Now before God this holy reuerent Frier 2457
All our whole Citie is much bound vnto, 2458
Goe tell the Countie presently of this, 2449
For I will haue this knot knit vp to morrow. 2450
Iul: Nurse, will you go with me to my Closet, 2459
To sort such things as shall be requisite 2460
Against to morrow. 2461
Moth: I pree thee doo, good Nurse goe in with her, 2463
Helpe her to sort Tyres, Rebatoes, Chaines, 2460
And I will come vnto you presently.
Nur: Come sweet hart, shall we goe e ⎫ 2463+
Iul: I pree thee let vs. ⎭

Exeunt Nurse and Iuliet. 2465

Moth: Me thinks on Thursday would be time enough. 2462
Capo: I say I will haue this dispatcht to morrow, 2464
Goe one and certefie the Count thereof. 2449
Moth: I pray my Lord, let it be Thursday, 2462
Capo: I say to morrow while shees in the mood. 2464
Moth: We shall be short in our prouision, 2466
Capo:

61

Cape: Let me alone for that, goe get you in,
Now before God my heart is paising light,
To see her thus conformed to our will.   *Exeunt.*

Enter Nurse, Iuliet.

Nur: Come, come, what need you anie thing else?
Iul: Nothing good Nurse, but leaue me to my selfe:
For I doo meane to lye alone to night,
  Nur: Well theres a cleane smocke vnder your pillow,
and so good night,   *Exit.*

Enter Mother.

Moth: What are you busie, doo you need my helpe?
Iul: No Madame, I desire to lye alone,
For I haue manie things to thinke vpon.
  Moth: Well then good night, be stirring *Iuliet,*
The Countie will be earlie here to morrow.   *Exit.*
Iul: Farewell, God knowes when wee shall meete a-
gaine.
Ah, I doo take a fearfull thing in hand.
What if this Potion should not worke at all,
Must I of force be married to the Countie?
This shall forbid it. Knife, lye thou there.
What if the Frier should giue me this drinke
To payson mee, for feare I should disclose
Our former marriage? Ah, I wrong him much,
He is a holy and religious Man:
I will not entertaine so bad a thought.
What if I should be stifled in the Toomb?

of Romeo and Iuliet.

Awake an houre before the appointed time:
Ah then I feare I shall be lunaticke,
And playing with my dead forefathers bones,
Dash out my franticke braines. Me thinkes I see
My Cosin *Tybalt* weltring in his bloud,
Seeking for *Romeo*: stay *Tybalt*, stay.
Romeo I come, this doe I drinke to thee.
        She fals upon her bed within the Curtaines.

        Enter Nurse with hearbs, Mother.

  Moth: Thats well said Nurse, set all in redines,
The Countie will be heere immediatly.

        Enter Oldman.
  Cap: Make hast, make hast, for it is almost day,
The Curfewe bell hath rung, 'tis foure a clocke,
Looke to your bakt meates good Angelica.
  Nur: Goe get you to bed you cotqueane, I faith you
will be sicke anone.
  Cap: I warrant thee Nurse, I haue ere now watcht all
night, and haue taken no harme at all.
  Moth: I you haue bene a mouse hunt in your time.

        Enter Seruingman with Logs & Coales.

  Cap: A Ielous hood, a Ielous hood: How now sirra?
What haue you there?
  Ser: Forsooth Logs.
  Cap: Goe, goe choose dryer. Will will tell thee where
thou shalt fetch them.
  Ser: Nay I warrant let me alone, I haue a heade I warrant to
                      choose

The excellent Tragedie.

choose a Log.

Exit.

Cap: Well goe thy way, thou shalt be logger head,
Come, come, make hast call vp your daughter,
The Countie will be heere with musicke straight;
Gods me hees come, Nurse call vp my daughter.

Nur: Goe, get you gone, What lambe, what Lady
birde, fast I warrant, What Iuliet? well, let the County take
you in your bed, yee sleepe for a weeke now, but the next
night, the Countie Paris hath set vp his rest that you shal rest
but little, What lambe I say, fast still; what Lady, Loue,
what bride, what Iuliet? Gods me how sound she sleepes, Nay
then I see I must wake you indeed. Whats heere, laide on
your bed, drest in your cloathes and down, ah me, alack the
day, some Aqua vitæ hoe.

Enter Mother.

Moth: How now whats the matter?
Nur: Alack the day, shees dead, shees dead, shees dead.
Moth: Accurst, vnhappy, miserable time.

Enter Oldeman.

Cap: Come, come, make hast, wheres my daughter?
Moth: Ah shees dead, shees dead.
Cap: Stay, let me see, all pale and wan.
Accursed time, vnfortunate olde man.

Enter Fryer and Paris.

Par: What is the bride ready to goe to Church?
Cap: Ready to goe, but neuer to returne.
O Sonne the night before thy wedding day,
Hath Death laine with thy bride, flower as she is,
Deflowerd by him, see, where she lyes,

Death

of Romeo and Iuliet.

Death is my Sonne in Law, to him I giue all that I haue.
   Par: Haue I thought long to see this mornings face,
And doth it now present such prodegies?
Accurst, vnhappy, miserable man,
Forlorne, forsaken, destitute I am;
Borne to the world to be a slaue in it.
Distrest, remediles, and vnfortunate.
O heauens, O nature, wherefore did you make me,
To liue so vile, so wretched as I shall.
   Cap: O heere she lies that was our hope, our ioy,
And being dead, dead sorrow nips vs all.

              All at once cry out and wring their hands.

   All cry: And all our ioy, and all our hope is dead,
Dead, lost, vndone, absented, wholy fled.
   Cap: Cruel, vniust, impartiall destinies,
Why to this day haue you preseru'd my life?
To see my hope, my stay, my ioy, my life,
Depriude of sence, of life, of all by death,
Cruell, vniust, impartiall destinies.
   Cap: O sad fac'd sorrow map of misery,
Why this sad time haue I desird to see.
This day, this vniust, this impartiall day
Wherein I hop'd to see my comfort full,
To be depriude by suddaine destinie.
   Moth: O woe, alacke, distrest, why should I liue?
To see this day, this miserable day.
Alacke the time that euer I was borne,
To be partaker of this destinie.
Alacke the day, alacke and welladay.
   Fr: O peace for shame, if not for charity,
Your daughter liues in peace and happines,
And it is vaine to wish it otherwise.

              I 2   Come

The excellent Tragedie

Come flie by yee Rosemary in this dead coarse,
And as the cuftome of our Country is,
In all her beft and fumptuous ornaments,
Conuay her where her Ancestors lie tomb'd,

Cap: Let it be so, come wofull sorrow-mates,
Let vs together taste this bitter fate.

They all but the Nurse goe foorth, casting Rosemary on her and shutting the Curtens.

Enter Mufitions.

Nur: Put vp, put vp, this is a wofull case.   *Exit.*
1. I by my troth Miftresse is it, it had need be mended.

Enter Seruingman.

Ser: Alack alack what shall I doe, come Fidlers play me some mery dumpe.
1. A sir, this is no time to play.
Ser: You will not then?
1. No marry will wee.
Ser: Then will I giue it you, and soundly to.
1. What will you giue vs?
Ser: The fidler, Ho're you, Ile fa you, Ile sol you.
1. If you re vs and fa vs, we will note you.
Ser: I will put vp my Iron dagger, and beate you with my wodden wit, Come on Simon found Pot, Ile pose you,
1. Lets heare.
Ser: When griping griefe the heart doth wound,
And dolefull dumps the minde oppresse,
Then musique with her siluer sound,
Why siluer sound? Why siluer sound?
1. I thinke because musicke hath a sweet sound.
Ser: Prettie, what say you Mathew minikine?

of Romeo and Iuliet.

3. I thinke because Musitions sound for siluer.
Ser: Prettie too: come, what say you?
3. I say nothing.
Ser: I thinke so, Ile speake for you because you are the Singer, I saye Siluer sound, because such Fellowes as you haue sildome Golde for sounding. Farewell Fidlers, farewell.   *Exit.*
1. Farewell and be hangd: come lets goe.   *Exeunt.*

Enter Romeo.

Rom: If I may trust the flattering Eye of Sleepe,
My Dreame presagde some good euent to come,
My bosome Lord sits chearfull in his throne,
And I am comforted with pleasing dreames.
Me thought I was this night alreadie dead:
(Strange dreames that giue a dead man leaue to thinke)
And that my Ladie *Iuliet* came to me,
And breathd such life with kisses in my lips,
That I reuiude and was an Emperour.

Enter Balthasar his man booted.

Newes from *Verona.* How now *Balthasar*,
How doth my Ladie? Is my Father well?
How fares my *Iuliet?* that I aske againe:
If she be well, then nothing can be ill.
  Balt: Then nothing can be ill, for she is well,
Her bodie sleepes in *Capels* Monument,
And her immortall parts with Angels dwell,
Pardon me Sir, that am the Messenger of such bad tidings.
  Rom: Is it euen so? then I defie my Starres.

I 3   Goe

67

The excellent Tragedie

2749–50	Goe get me incke and paper, hyre post horse,
2750	I will not stay in *Mantua* to night.
2750+	*Balt:* Pardon me Sir, I will not leaue yeu thus,
2752	Your lookes are dangerous and full of feare:
2752+	I dare not, nor I will not leaue you yet.
2755, 2749	*Rom:* Doe as I bid thee, get me incke and paper,
2760, 2759	And hyre those horse: stay not I say.
2758	*Exit Baltbesar.*
2761	Well *Iuliet*, I will lye with thee to night.
2762	Lets see for meanes. As I doe remember
2764–5	Here dwells a Pothecarie whom oft I noted
2769	As I past by, whose needie shop is stufft
2772	With beggerly accounts of emptie boxes:
2770	And in the same an *Aligarta* hangs,
2774	Olde endes of packthred, and cakes of Roses,
	Are thinly strewed to make vp a show.
	Him as I noted, thus with my selfe I thought:
	And if a man should need a payson now,
2778	(Whose present sale is death in *Mantua*)
2779–80	Here he might buy it. This thought of mine
2780, 2765	Did but forerunne my need: and here about he dwells.
2783	Being Holiday the Beggers shop is shut.
	What ho Apothecarie, come forth I say.
2785	*Enter Apothecarie.*
2786	*Apo:* VVho calls, what would you sir?
2788	*Rom:* Heeres twentie duckates,
2788–9	Giue me a dram of some such speeding geere,
2790–1	As will dispatch the wearie takers life,
2793	As suddenly as powder being fierd
	From forth a Cannons mouth.
2795	*Apo:* Such drugs I haue I must of force confesse,
2795–6	But yet the law is death to those that sell them.
	Rom:

2050

2060

2070

of Romeo and Iuliet.

Rom: Art thou so bare and full of pouertie,
And doost thou feare to violate the Law?
The Law is not thy frend, nor the Lawes frend,
And therefore make no conscience of the law:
Vpon thy backe hangs ragged Miserie,
And starued Famine dwelleth in thy cheekes.
　Apo: My pouertie but not my will consents.
　Rom: I pay thy pouertie, but not thy will.
　Apo: Hold take you this, and put it in anie liquid thing
you will, and it will serue had you the liues of twenty men.
　Rom: Hold, take this gold, worse poyson to mens soules
Than this which thou hast giuen me. Goe hye thee hence,
Goe buy thee cloathes, and get thee into flesh.
Come cordiall and not poyson, goe with mee
To *Iuliets* Graue: for there must I vse thee.　　*Exeunt.*

Enter Frier Iohn.

　Iohn: VVhat Frier *Laurence*, Brother, ho?
　Laur: This same should be the voyce of Frier *Iohn.*
VVhat newes from *Mantua*, what will *Romeo* come?
　Iohn: Going to seeke a barefoote Brother out,
One of our order to associate mee,
Here in this Cittie visiting the sick,
VVhereas the infectious pestilence remaind:
And being by the Searchers of the Towne
Found and examinde, we were both shut vp.
　Laur: VVho bare my letters then to *Romeo?*
　Iohn: I haue them still, and here they are.
　Laur: Now by my holy Order,
The letters were not nice, but of great weight.
Goe get thee hence, and get me presently

The excellent Tragedie

A spade and mattocke.

John: Well I will presently go fetch thee them. *Exit.*

Laur: Now must I to the Monument alone,
Least that the Ladie should before I come
Be wakde from sleepe. I will hye
To free her from that Tombe of miserie. *Exit.*

Enter Countie Paris and his Page with flowers and sweete water.

Par: Put out the torch, and lye thee all along
Vnder this Ew-tree, keeping thine eare close to the hollow
     ground:
And if thou heare one tread within this Churchyard,
Steight giue me notice.
     Boy: I will my Lord.

Paris strewes the Tomb with flowers.

Par: Sweete Flower, with flowers I strew thy Bridale
     bed:
Sweete Tombe that in thy circuite dost containe,
The perfect modell of eternitie:
Faire *Iuliet* that with Angells dost remaine,
Accept this latest fauour at my hands,
That liuing honourd thee, and being dead
With funerall praises doo adorne thy Tombe.
     Boy whistles and calls. My Lord.

Enter Romeo and Balthasar, with a torch, a mattocke, and a crow of yron.

                                                    Par:

of Romeo and Iulet.

Par: The boy giues warning, something doth approach,
What cursed foote wanders this wayes to night,
To stay my obsequies and true loues rites?
What with a torch, muffle me night a while,
   Rom: Giue mee this mattocke, and this wrentching Iron.
And take these letters, early in the morning,
See thou deliuer them to my Lord and Father,
So get thee gone and trouble me no more,
Why I descend into this bed of death,
Is partly to behold my Ladies face:
But chiefly to take from her dead finger,
A precious ring which I must vse
In deare imployment, but if thou wilt stay,
Further to prie in what I vndertake,
By heauen Ile teare thee ioynt by ioynt,
And strewe thys hungry churchyard with thy limmes,
The time and my intents are sauage, wilde.
   Balt: Well, Ile be gone and not trouble you.
   Rom: So shalt thou win my fauour, take thou this,
Commend me to my Father, farwell good fellow,
   Balt: Yet for all this will I not part from hence.
How oft haue many at the houre of death
Beene blith and pleasant, which their keepers call
Romeo opens the tombe.
A lightning before death. But how may
   Rom: Thou detestable maw, thou womb of death,
Gorde with the dearest morsell of the earth,
Thus I enforce thy rotten iawes to ope,
   Par: This is that banisht haughtie Mountague,
That murdred my loues cosen, I will apprehend him.
Stop thy vnhallowed toyle vile Mountague,
Can vengeance be pursued further then death?
I doe attach thee as a fellon heere,
The Law condemnes thee, therefore thou must dye.
   Rom: I must indeed, and therefore came I hither,
Good youth begon, tempt not a desperate man,
     K   Heape

The excellent Tragedie

Heape not another sinne vpon my head
By sheding of thy bloud, I doo protest
I loue thee better then I loue my selfe,
For I come hyther armde against my selfe,
  Par: I doe defie thy coniurations:
And doe attach thee as a fellon heere.
  Rom: What dost thou tempt me, then haue at thee boy.

They fight.

  Boy: O Lord they fight, I will goe call the watch.
  Par: Ah I am slaine, if thou be mercifull
Open the tombe, lay me with *Iuliet*.
  Rom: Yfaith I will, let me peruse this face,
Mercutios kinsman, noble County *Paris* ?
What said my man, when my betossed soule
Did not regard him as we past along,
Did he not say *Paris* should haue maried
Iuliet ? eyther he said so, or I dreamd it so.
But I will satisfie thy last request,
For thou hast prizd thy loue aboue thy life,
Death lye thou there, by a dead man interd,
How oft haue many at the houre of death
Beene blith and pleasant? which their keepers call
A lightning before death But how may I
Call this a lightning. Ah deare *Iuliet*,
How well thy beauty doth become this graue?
O I beleeue that vnsubstanciall death,
Is amorous, and doth court my loue.
Therefore will I, O heere, O euer heere,
Set vp my euerlasting rest
With wormes, that are thy chambermayds.
Come desperate Pilot now at once runne on
The dashing rockes thy sea-sicke weary barge,
Heere to my loue. O true Apothecary!
Thy drugs are swift: thus with a kisse I dye.

Falls.
Enter

of Romeo and Iuliet.

Enter Fryer with a Lanthorne.

How oft to night haue these my aged feete
Stumbled at graues as I did passe along.
Whose there?
   Man. A frend and one that knowes you well.
    Fr: Who is it that consorts so late the dead,
What light is yon? if I be not deceiued,
Me thinkes it burnes in *Capels* monument?
   Man. It doth so holy Sir, and there is one
That loues you dearely.
   Fr. Who is it?
   Man. Romeo.
   Fr: How long hath he beene there?
   Man: Full halfe an houre and more.
   Fr: Goe with me thether.
   Man: I dare not sir, he knowes not I am heere:
On paine of death he chargde me to be gone,
And not for to disturbe him in his enterprize.
   Fr: Then must I goe : my minde presageth ill.

Fryer stoops and lookes on the blood and weapons.

What bloud is this that staines the entrance
Of this marble stony monument?
What meanes these maisterles and goory weapons?
Ah me I doubt, whose heere? what *Romeo* dead?
Who and *Paris* too? what vnluckie houre
Is accessary to so foule a sinne?

                                        Iuliet rises.
The Lady sturres.
                    K   *Iul:*

The excellent Tragedie

Ah comfortable Fryer,
I doe remember well where I should be,
And what we talkt of: but yet I cannot see
Him for whose sake I vndertooke this hazard.
  Fri. Lady come foorth, I heare some noise at hand,
We shall be taken, *Paris* he is slaine,
And *Romeo* dead: and if we heere be tane
We shall be thought to be as accessarie:
I will prouide for you in some close Nunery.
  Iuli. Ah leaue me, leaue me, I will not from hence.
  Fri. I heare some noise, I dare not stay, come, come.
  Iul. Goe get thee gone.
Whats heere a cup closde in my louers hands?
Ah churle drinke all, and leaue no drop for me.

              Enter watch.
  Watch: This way, this way.
  Iul: I, noise? then must I be resolute,
O happy dagger thou shalt end my feare,
Rest in my bosome, thus I come to thee.
            She stabs herselfe and falles.

  Cap: Come looke about, what weapons haue we heere?
See frends whose *Iuliet* two daies buried,
New bleeding wounded, search and see who's neare,
Attach and bring them to vs presently.
            Enter one with the Fryer.
  1. Captaine heere a Fryer with tooles about him,
Fitte to ope a tombe.
  Cap: A great suspition, keep him safe.

of Romeo and Iuliet.

Enter one with Romeos Man.

1. Heeres *Romeos* Man.
Capt: Keepe him to be examinde.

Enter Prince with others.

Prin: What early mischiefe calls vs vp so soone.
Capt: O noble Prince, see here
Where *Iuliet* that hath lyen intoombd two dayes,
Warme and fresh bleeding, *Romeo* and Countie *Paris*
Likewise newly slaine.
Prin: Search seeke about to finde the murderers.

Enter olde Capolet and his Wife.

Capo: What rumor's this that is so early vp?
Moth: The people in the streetes crie *Romeo*,
And some on *Iuliet*: as if they alone
Had been the cause of such a mutinie.
Capo: See Wife, this dagger hath mistooke:
For (loe) the backe is emptie of yong *Mountague*,
And it is sheathed in our Daughters breast.

Enter olde Mountague.

Prin: Come *Mountague*, for thou art early vp,
To see thy Sonne and Heire more early downe.
Mount: Dread Souereigne, my Wife is dead to night,
And yong *Bennolio* is deceased too:
What further mischiefe can there yet be found?
Prin: First come and see, then speake.
Mount: O thou vntaught, what manners is in this
To presse before thy Father to a graue.
Prin: Come seale your mouthes of outrage for a while,
And let vs seeke to finde the Authors out
Of such a hainous and seld seene mischaunce.
Bring forth the parties in suspition.
Fr: I am the greatest able to doo least,
Most worthie Prince, heare me but speake the truth,

K 3   And

The excellent Tragedie

And Ile Informe you how these things fell out.
Iuliet here slaine was married to that Romeo,
Without her Fathers or her Mothers grant:
The Nurse was priuie to the marriage.
The balefull day of this vnhappie marriage,
VVas Tybalts doomesday: for which Romeo
VVas banished from hence to Mantua.
He gone, her Father sought by foule constraint
To marrie her to Paris: But her Soule
(Loathing a second Contract) did refuse
To giue consent, and therefore did she vrge me
Either to finde a meanes she might auoyd
VVhat so her Father sought to force her too:
Or els all desperately she threatned
Euen in my presence to dispatch her selfe.
Then did I giue her, (tutord by mine arte)
A potion that should make her seeme as dead:
And told her that I would with all post speed
Send hence to Mantua for her Romeo,
That he might come and take her from the Toombe.
But he that had my Letters (Frier Iohn)
Seeking a Brother to associate him,
VVhereas the sicke infection remaind,
VVas stayed by the Searchers of the Towne,
But Romeo vnderstanding by his man,
That Iuliet was deceasde, returnde in post
Vnto Verona for to see his loue,
VVhat after happened touching Paris death,
Or Romeos is to me vnknowne at all.
But when I came to take the Lady hence,
I found them dead, and she awakt from sleep:
VVhom faine I would haue taken from the tombe,
VVhich she refused seeing Romeo dead,
Anone I heard the watch and then I fled,
VVhat's after happened I am ignorant of,
And if in this ought haue miscaried.

of Romeo and Iuliet.

By me, or by my meanes let my old life
Be sacrificed some houre before his time,
To the most strickest rigor of the Law.

    Pry: VVe still haue knowne thee for a holy man,
VVheres *Romeos* man, what can he say in this?

    Balth: I brought my maister word that shee was dead,
And then he poasted straight from *Mantua*,
Vnto this Toombe. These Letters he deliuered me,
Charging me early giue them to his Father.

    Prin: Lets see the Letters, I will read them ouer.
VVhere is the Counties Boy that calld the VVatch?

    Boy: I brought my Master vnto *Iuliets* graue,
But one approaching, straight I calld my Master,
At last they fought, I ran to call the VVatch.
And this is all that I can say or know.

    Prin: These letters doe make good the Fryers wordes,
Come *Capulet*, and come olde *Mountagewe*,
VVhere are these enemies? see what hate hath done.

    Cap: Come brother *Mountague* giue me thy hand,
There is my daughters dowry: for now no more
Can I bestowe on her, thats all I haue.

    Moun: But I will giue them more, I will erect
Her statue of pure golde:
That while *Verona* by that name is knowne,
There shall no statue of such price be set,
As that of *Romeos* loued *Iuliet*.

    Cap: As rich shall *Romeo* by his Lady lie,
Poore Sacrifices to our Enmitie.

    Prin: A gloomie peace this day doth with it bring,
Come, let vs hence,
To haue more talke of these sad things,
Some shall be pardoned and some punished:
For nere was heard a Storie of more woe,
Than this of *Iuliet* and her *Romeo*.

FINIS.

Signature	Page Number	Quarto Through Line Numbers	Riverside Edition
A3ʳ	3	13–25	Prologue, 1–14
A4ʳ	5	26–51	I.i.1–24
A4ᵛ	6	52–81	I.i.25–59, 63 S.D.–78 S.D., 81–91, 96
B1ʳ	7	82–113	I.i.97–107, 116–29, 141–3, 155 S.D., 144, 156–7
B1ᵛ	8	114–45	I.i.158–85
B2ʳ	9	146–77	I.i.186–216; I.ii. S.D., 4
B2ᵛ	10	178–209	I.ii.5–38
B3ʳ	11	210–41	I.ii.39–69
B3ᵛ	12	242–73	I.ii.69–100
B4ʳ	13	274–305	I.ii.101–I.iii.31
B4ᵛ	14	306–38	I.iii.32–68, 74–8, 96–9 S.D.
C1ʳ	15	339–70	I.iii.100–3, I.iv.1–16, 29–43
C1ᵛ	16	371–402	I.iv.44–77
C2ʳ	17	403–34	I.iv.78–111
C2ᵛ	18	435–66	I.iv.112–13; I.v.15 S.D., 16–49
C3ʳ	19	467–98	I.v.50–82
C3ᵛ	20	499–530	I.v.82–115
C4ʳ	21	531–62	I.v.115–24; III.iv.6–7, 33; I.v.128–44
C4ᵛ	22	563–93	II.i.1–32
D1ʳ	23	594–625	II.i.32–42; II.ii.1–24
D1ᵛ	24	626–57	II.ii.25–56
D2ʳ	25	658–89	II.ii.57–88
D2ᵛ	26	690–721	II.ii.89–118
D3ʳ	27	722–53	II.ii.119–20, 136–48, 156–70
D3ᵛ	28	754–85	II.ii.171–89; II.iii.1–8, 15–17
D4ʳ	29	786–817	II.iii.18–49
D4ᵛ	30	818–49	II.iii.50–81
E1ʳ	31	850–83	II.iii.82–92; II.iv.1–20
E1ᵛ	32	884–919	II.iv.21–62
E2ʳ	33	920–53	II.iv.62–102
E2ᵛ	34	954–89	II.iv.103–44
E3ʳ	35	990–1025	II.iv.145–81, 186–90
E3ᵛ	36	1026–59	II.iv.191–217; II.v.1–60
E4ʳ	37	1060–94	II.v.60–78; II.vi.1–20
E4ᵛ	38	1095–1128	II.vi.24–37; III.i.1–25
F1ʳ	39	1129–62	III.i.26–76

Signature	Page Number	Quarto Through Line Numbers	Riverside Edition
F1^v	40	1163–97	III.i.77–113
F2^r	41	1198–1225	III.i.114–39
F2^v	42	1226–59	III.i.139–79
F3^r	43	1260–92	III.i.180–97; III.ii.1–4, 31 S.D., 34–56
F3^v	44	1293–1328	III.ii.57–128
F4^r	45	1329–63	III.ii.129–31, 140–3; III.iii.1–26
F4^v	46	1364–99	III.iii.27–64
G1^r	47	1400–30	III.iii.65–92
G1^v	48	1431–65	III.iii.93–144
G2^r	49	1466–93	III.iii.145–75; III.iv.1–2
G2^v	50	1494–1523	III.iv.3–35
G3^r	51	1524–53	III.v.1–29
G3^v	52	1554–84	III.v.30–67 S.D.,
G4^r	53	1585–1614	III.v.67 S.D.–112
G4^v	54	1615–48	III.v.113–55
H1^r	55	1649–83	III.v.156–89
H1^v	56	1684–1719	III.v.190–233
H2^r	57	1720–47	III.v.234–42; IV.i.1–16
H2^v	58	1748–80	IV.i.17–48
H3^r	59	1781–1816	IV.i.49–96
H3^v	60	1817–43	IV.i.96–126; IV.ii.1–14
H4^r	61	1844–73	IV.ii.14 S.D.–38
H4^v	62	1874–1900	IV.ii.42–47; IV.iii.1–33
I1^r	63	1901–27	IV.iii.31–58; IV.iv.1–18
I1^v	64	1928–57	IV.iv.18–28; IV.v.1–37
I2^r	65	1958–89	IV.v.38–68
I2^v	66	1990–2019	IV.v.79–133
I3^r	67	2020–47	IV.v.134–46; V.i.1–24
I3^v	68	2048–79	V.i.25–67
I4^r	69	2080–2109	V.i.68–86; V.ii.1–21
I4^v	70	2110–35	V.ii.21–30; V.iii.1–17 S.D., 21 S.D.
K1^r	71	2136–69	V.iii.18–21, 22–59
K1^v	72	2170–2203	V.iii.62–120 S.D.
K2^r	73	2204–31	V.iii.120 S.D.–147
K2^v	74	2232–60	V.iii.148–87
K3^r	75	2261–93	V.iii.181 S.D.–223
K3^v	76	2294–2329	V.iii.230–67
K4^r	77	2330–64	V.iii.267–310

APPENDIX

Supplementary pages from the copy in the Library of Trinity College Cambridge, reproduced by kind permission of the Master and Fellows of Trinity College.

The most excellent Tragedie,

Rom: Nay thats not so. *Mer:* I meane sir in delay,
We burne our lights by night, like Lampes by day,
Take our good meaning for our iudgement sits
Three times a day, ere once in her right wits.
 Rom: So we meane well by going to this maske:
But tis no wit to goe.
 Mer: Why *Romeo* may one aske?
 Rom: I dreamt a dreame to night.
 Mer: And so did I. *Rom:* Why what was yours?
 Mer: That dreamers often lie. (true,
 Rom: In bed a sleepe while they doe dreame things
 Mer: Ah then I see Queene Mab hath bin with you.
 Ben: Queene Mab whats she?
She is the Fairies Midwife and doth come
In shape no bigger than an Aggat stone,
On the forefinger of a Burgomaster,
Drawne with a teeme of little Atomi,
Athwart mens noses when they lie a sleepe.
Her waggon spokes are made of spinners webs,
The couer, of the winges of Grashoppers,
The traces are the Moone-shine watrie beames,
The collers crickets bones, the lash of filmes,
Her waggoner is a small gray coated flie,
Not halfe so big as is a little worme,
Pickt from the lasie finger of a maide,
And in this sort she gallops vp and downe
Through Louers braines, and then they dream of loue:
O're Courtiers knees: who strait on cursies dreame
O're Ladies lips, who dreame on kisses straite:
Which oft the angrie Mab with blisters plagues,
Because their breathes with sweet meats tainted are:
Sometimes she gallops ore a Lawers lap,
                                                And

The most excellent Tragedie,

Ca: Goe too, you are a saucie knaue.
This tricke will scath you one day I know what,
Well said my hartes. Be quiet:
More light Ye knaue, or I will make you quiet.

Tibalt: Patience perforce with wilfull choller mee-
Makes my flesh tremble in their different greetings: (ting,
I will withdraw, but this intrusion shall
Now seeming sweet, conuert to bitter gall.

Rom: If I prophane with my vnworthie hand,
This holie shrine, the gentle sinne is this:
My lips two blushing Pilgrims ready stand,
To smooth the rough touch with a gentle kisse.

Iuli: Good Pilgrime you doe wrong your hand, too
Which mannerly deuotion shewes in this: (much,
For Saints haue hands which holy Palmers touch,
And Palme to Palme is holy Palmers kisse.

Rom: Haue not Saints lips, and holy Palmers too?

Iuli: Yes Pilgrime lips that they must vse in praier.

Ro: Why then faire saint, let lips do what hands doo,
They pray, yeeld thou, least faith turne to dispaire.

Iu: Saints doe not mooue though, grant nor praier
forsake.

Ro: Then mooue not till my praiers effect I take.
Thus from my lips, by yours my sin is purgde.

Iu: Then haue my lips the sin that they haue tooke.

Ro: Sinne from my lips, O trespasse sweetly vrgde!
Giue me my sinne againe.

Iu: You kisse by the booke.

Nurse: *Madame your mother calles.*

Rom: What is her mother?

Nurse: *Marrie Batcheler her mother is the Ladie of the*
house, and a good Lady, and a wise, and a vertuous, I nurst
her

The most excellent Tragedie,

Enter Romeo alone.

Ro: Shall I goe forward and my heart is here?
Turne backe dull earth and finde thy Center out.

Enter Benuolio Mercutio.

Ben: Romeo, my cosen *Romeo.*

Mer: Doest thou heare he is wise,
Vpon my life he hath stolne him home to bed.

Ben: He came this way, and leapt this Orchard wall.
Call good *Mercutio.*

Mer: Call, nay Ile coniure too.
Romeo, madman, humors, passion, liuer, appeare thou in
likenes of a sigh: speak but one rime & I am satisfied, cry
but ay me. Pronounce but Loue and Doue, speake to
my gossip *Venus* one faire word, one nickname for her
purblinde sonne and heire young *Abraham: Cupid* hee
that shot so trim when young King *Cophetua* loued the
begger wench. Hee heares me not. I coniure thee by
Rosalindes bright eye, high forehead, and scarlet lip, her
prettie foote, straight leg, and quiuering thigh, and the
demaines that there adiacent lie, that in thy likenesse
thou appeare to vs.

Ben: If he doe heare thee thou wilt anger him.

Mer: Tut this cannot anger him, marrie if one shuld
raise a spirit in his Mistris circle of some strange fashion,
making it there to stand till she had laid it, and coniurde
it downe, that were some spite. My inuocation is faire
and honest, and in his Mistris name I coniure onely but
to raise vp him.

Ben: Well he hath hid himselfe amongst those trees,
To be consorted with the humerous night,
Blinde in his loue, and best befits the darke.

Mer:

The excellent Tragedie

And turnd that blacke word death to banishment:
This is meere mercie, and thou seest it not.
  Rom: Tis torture and not mercie, heauen is heere
Where *Iuliet* liues: and euerie cat and dog,
And little mouse, euerie vnworthie thing
Liue here in heauen, and may looke on her,
But *Romeo* may not. More validitie,
More honourable state, more courtship liues
In carrion flyes, than *Romeo*: they may seaze
On the white wonder of faire *Iuliets* skinne,
And steale immortall kisses from her lips;
But *Romeo* may not, he is banished.
Flies may doo this, but I from this must flye.
Oh Father hadst thou no strong poyson mixt,
No sharpe ground knife, no present meane of death,
Though nere so meane, but banishment
To torture me withall: ah, banished.
O Frier, the damned vse that word in hell:
Howling attends it. How hadst thou the heart,
Being a Diuine, a ghostly Confessor,
A sinne absoluer, and my frend profest,
To mangle me with that word, Banishment?
  Fr: Thou fond mad man, heare me but speake a word.
  Rom: O, thou wilt talke againe of Banishment.
  Fr: Ile giue thee armour to beare off this word,
Aduersities sweete milke, philosophie,
To comfort thee though thou be banished.
  Rom: Yet Banished? hang vp philosophie,
Vnlesse philosophie can make a *Iuliet*,
Displant a Towne, reuerse a Princes doome,
It helpes not, it preuailes not, talke no more.
  Fr: O, now I see that madmen haue no eares.
  Rom: How should they, when that wise men haue no
eyes.
  Fr: Let me dispute with thee of thy estate.
  Rom: Thou canst not speak of what thou dost not feele.
Wert

The excellent Tragedie

Enter Paris.

Heere comes the Lady to my cell,
  Par: Welcome my loue, my Lady and my wife:
  Iu: That may be sir, when I may be a wife.
  Par: That may be, must be loue, on thursday next.
  Iu: What must be shalbe.
  Fr: Thats a certaine text.
  Par: What come ye to confession to this Fryer.
  Iu: To tell you that were to confesse to you.
  Par: Do not deny to him that you loue me.
  Iul: I will confesse to you that I loue him,
  Par: So I am sure you will that you loue me.
  Iu: And if I doe, it wilbe of more price,
Being spoke behinde your backe, than to your face.
  Par: Poore soule thy face is much abus'd with teares.
  Iu: The teares haue got small victory by that,
For it was bad enough before their spite.
  Par: Thou wrongst it more than teares by that report.
  Iu: That is no wrong sir, that is a truth:
And what I spake I spake it to my face.
  Par: Thy face is mine and thou hast slaundred it.
  Iu: It may be so, for it is not mine owne.
Are you at leasure holy Father now:
Or shall I come to you at euening Masse?
  Fr: My leasure serues me pensiue daughter now,
My Lord we must entreate the time alone.
  Par: God sheild I should disturbe deuotion,
Iuliet farwell, and keep this holy kisse.

Exit Paris.

  Iu: Goe shut the doore and when thou hast done so,
Come weepe with me that am past cure, past help,
  Fr: Ah *Iuliet* I already know thy griefe,
I heare thou must and nothiug may proroge it,

H   On

The excellent Tragedie

A spade and mattocke.

Iohn: Well I will presently go fetch thee them. *Exit.*
Laur: Now must I to the Monument alone,
Least that the Ladie should before I come
Be wakde from sleepe. I will hye
To free her from that Tombe of miserie. *Exit.*

Enter Countie Paris and his Page with flowers and sweete Water.

Par: Put out the torch, and lye thee all along
Vnder this Ew-tree, keeping thine eare close to the hollow
  ground.
And if thou heare one tread within this Churchyard,
Staight giue me notice.
Boy: I will my Lord.

Paris strewes the Tomb with flowers.

Par: Sweete Flower, with flowers I strew thy Bridale
  bed:
Sweete Tombe that in thy circuite dost containe,
The perfect modell of eternitie:
Faire *Iuliet* that with Angells dost remaine,
Accept this latest fauour at my hands,
That liuing honourd thee, and being dead
With funerall praises doo adorne thy Tombe.
Boy whistles and calls. My Lord.

Enter Romeo and Balthasar, with a torch, a mattocke, and a crow of yron.

Par:

of Romeo and Iuliet.

Par: The boy giues warning, something doth approach,
What cursed foote wanders this was to night,
To stay my obsequies and true loues rites?
What with a torch, muffle me night a while.

Rom: Giue mee this mattocke, and this wrentching I-
ron.
And take these letters, early in the morning,
See thou deliuer them to my Lord and Father.
So get thee gone and trouble me no more.
Why I descend into this bed of death,
Is partly to behold my Ladies face,
But chiefly to take from her dead finger,
A precious ring which I must vse
In deare imployment: but if thou wilt stay,
Further to prie in what I vndertake,
By heauen Ile teare thee ioynt by ioynt,
And strewe thys hungry churchyard with thy lims.
The time and my intents are sauage, wilde.

Balt: Well, Ile be gone and not trouble you.

Rom: So shalt thou win my fauour, take thou this,
Commend me to my Father, farwell good fellow.

Balt: Yet, for all this will I not part from hence.

Romeo opens the tombe.

Rom: Thou detestable maw, thou womb of death,
Gorde with the dearest morsell of the earth.
Thus I enforce thy rotten iawes to ope.

Par: This is that banisht haughtie *Mountague*,
That murderd my loues cosen, I will apprehend him.
Stop thy vnhallowed toyle vile *Mountague*.
Can vengeance be pursued further then death?
I doe attach thee as a fellon heere.
The Law condemnes thee, therefore thou must dye,

Rom: I must indeed, and therefore came I hither,
Good youth be gone, tempt not a desperate man.

K   Heape

The excellent Tragedie

Heape not another sinne vpon my head
By sheding of thy bloud, I doe protest
I loue thee better then I loue my selfe:
For I come hyther armde against my selfe,
   Par: I doe defie thy coniurations:
And doe attach thee as a fellon heere.
   Rom: What dost thou tempt me, then haue at thee boy,

They fight.

   Boy: O Lord they fight, I will goe call the watch.
   Par: Ah I am slaine, if thou be mercifull
Open the tombe, lay me with *Iuliet.*
   Rom: Yfaith I will, let me peruse this face,
Mercutios kinsman, noble County *Paris?*
What said my man, when my betossed soule
Did not regard him as we past a long.
Did he not say *Paris* should haue maried
Iuliet? eyther he said so, or I dreamd it so.
But I will satisfie thy last request,
For thou hast prizd thy loue aboue thy life.
Death lye thou there, by a dead man interd,
How oft haue many at the houre of death
Beene blith and pleasant? which their keepers call
A lightning before death But how may I
Call this a lightning. Ah deare *Iuliet,*
How well thy beauty doth become this graue?
O I beleeue that vnsubstanciall death,
Is amorous, and doth court my loue.
Therefore will I, O heere, O euer heere,
Set vp my euerlasting rest
With wormes, that are thy chambermayds.
Come desperate Pilot now at once runne on
The dashing rockes thy sea-sicke weary barge.
Heers to my loue. O true Apothecary:
Thy drugs are swift; thus with a kisse I dye. *Falls.*
                                                            Enter

The excellent Tragedie

Ah comfortable Fryer.
I doe remember well where I should be,
And what we talkt of: but yet I cannot see
Him for whose sake I vndertooke this hazard.
　Fr: Lady come foorth, I heare some noise at hand,
We shall be taken, *Paris* he is slaine,
And *Romeo* dead: and if we heere be tane
We shall be thought to be as accessarie.
I will prouide for you in some close Nunery.
　Iul: Ah leaue me, leaue me, I will not from hence.
　Fr: I heare some noise, I dare not stay, come, come.
　Iul: Goe get thee gone.
Whats heere a cup closde in my louers hands?
Ah churle drinke all, and leaue no drop for me.

　　　　　　　Enter watch.
Watch: This way, this way.
Iul: I, noise? then must I be resolute.
O happy dagger thou shalt end my feare,
Rest in my bosome, thus I come to thee.
　　　　　She stabs herselfe and falles.

　　　　　　　Enter watch.

Cap: Come looke about, what weapons haue we heere?
See frends where *Iuliet* two daies buried,
New bleeding wounded, search and see who's neare,
Attach and bring them to vs presently.
　　　　　Enter one with the Fryer.
　1. Captaine heers a Fryer with tooles about him,
Fitte to ope a tombe.
　Cap: A great suspition, keep him safe.
　　　　　　　　　　　　　　　　Enter